The Burial of Jesus

History & Faith

James F. McGrath

WIPF & STOCK · Eugene, Oregon

Wipf and Stock Publishers
199 W 8th Ave, Suite 3
Eugene, OR 97401

The Burial of Jesus
History & Faith
By McGrath, James F.

Softcover ISBN-13: 978-1-6667-8415-2
Hardcover ISBN-13: 978-1-6667-8416-9
eBook ISBN-13: 978-1-6667-8417-6
Publication date 9/5/2023
Previously published by Patheos Press, 2012

Table of Contents

Acknowledgements

Just as no book comes about as the result of a single person's efforts without assistance and influences, so also no acknowledgments page does justice to the thanks due to those involved. The author wishes to thank his sister Rose and wife Elena for feedback on an earlier draft of the book, as well as students, friends, colleagues, blog readers, and other readers of drafts or of the first edition too numerous to name, indeed anyone who may have interacted with the author on various aspects of this topic. As always must be emphasized, any shortcomings are entirely the responsibility of the author. The cover photo was taken by Doug Chaplin, and the author is grateful for permission to use it.

Chapter 1
Introduction

Readers of this book will be aware of the claims that have appeared in the media since early 2007, to the effect that the tomb of Jesus and Mary Magdalene, together with their son Judas and other family members, had been discovered in the Talpiot neighborhood in Jerusalem. The existence of this tomb was not news to historians, archaeologists and Biblical scholars, since it had been discovered decades earlier, but it was highlighted by a television documentary and accompanying book, which brought to public attention once again the question of how faith and history relate to one another, as well as the question of how non-specialists are to assess claims that appear in the media about artifacts and evidence supposedly from Biblical times.

Many Christian believers reacted dismissively to reports about the Talpiot tomb. Yet this was not because they were aware of the problems that scholars and historians were pointing out with the evidence and its interpretation as presented in the documentary or other outlets. Rather, it was because of a prior assumption that, since they "know" what happened because it is described in the Bible, they can safely ignore as either a hoax or a mistake any evidence that seems to run counter to their understanding of a given Biblical story. Some even found themselves wondering how anyone could be so audacious as to claim that a tomb had been found where Jesus' bones rested long after Easter, and why historians would consider it legitimate to investigate and discuss ideas so antithetical to Christian faith. The impression many Christian believers end up with is that historians are a bunch of atheists and unbelievers, out to discredit and undermine their faith at all costs.

This impression is inevitably true of *some* who work in the field of history, just as it is true of some biologists and some musicians and even some preachers, but there is no reason to think that it is true of *the majority* of scholars working in any of these fields. Indeed, there is much evidence to refute it, much evidence that there are many people working in the fields of history and Biblical studies as an *expression of their faith* rather than because of opposition to it. One reason why some get a mistaken impression about this is a failure to understand how historical inquiry works, how it investigates questions about the past, how it evaluates evidence, and how it draws conclusions.

This book will seek to clarify precisely what historical study involves, and will argue that the very common approach of taking Biblical stories uncritically at face value, and using them as a reason for dismissing evidence not only from history but from science and other sources of knowledge, is fundamentally misguided. Historical study provides us with the only tools available to us for knowing about the past. Obviously there are sub-disciplines such as archaeology that must be mentioned alongside the study of texts and historical records. There are likewise scientific methods (such as forensics and radiometric dating) that can be used to aid historical inquiry. All of these, however, can be considered components of, or tools to be put to use in the service of, historical investigation. If we cast aside these methods of studying the past, the weighing of evidence and drawing of conclusions through a process of deductive logic and inference, then we are left with the stories that are told in texts, and one can do nothing more than simply accept or reject them by a leap of faith.

Although this latter option might seem viable to some religious believers, in fact it is anything but. The truthfulness of one's own religious texts may seem obvious to someone raised in a given tradition or whose life has been transformed in connection with those writings. This is, however, equally true of those raised in, or whose lives have been transformed by, some other tradition, in which they read a very different set of Scriptures. Very few of those who emphasize the need to accept Biblical narratives as truthful purely on the basis of faith alone will grant the legitimacy of those who do the same in relation to the Book of Mormon or the Qur'an. And if one wants to assess and evaluate competing claims about the past, then one has to have tools to use and ground rules that are generally agreed upon by all participants, irrespective of what their religious tradition may be or whether they have one at all.

The tools in question are the methods of historical study, and they work precisely because they proceed by assessing evidence in a way that, while not capable of being completely unbiased or impartial, can nonetheless be considered fair, and which treats all sources and all claims about the past on an equal basis, holding them to the same standard of evidence. Particularly for Christians, for whom past events are central to their religious beliefs and doctrines, history is important and cannot be ignored.

This book offers an introduction to how historical study works, and will suggest ways in which the fruits of historical study can be integrated into Christian faith and theology, with particular focus on the example of what we can know from texts and archaeology about matters such as the tomb and burial of Jesus. The reasons for focusing on this particular subject are many, and include the recent claims about the burial of Jesus mentioned earlier, the general neglect of the subject in many studies that are in a hurry to get from the crucifixion to the resurrection, and the crucial importance of understanding the burial of Jesus if we are to make sense of the rise of Christian faith in his resurrection.

Since historical study, as we shall see, needs to ask critical questions about how much we know and with what degree of certainty, this book addresses not only the burial and resurrection of Jesus, but more broadly the subject of faith and doubt. It will be argued that these should be understood not as opposites but as necessary partners in approaching this (and perhaps any) subject within the framework of Christianity. Faith, taken to its extreme, becomes credulity, gullibility, and willingness to believe anything, to accept uncritically things that we are told by the "right" book or the "right" person. Although such faith has never been healthy, and never been what the Bible means by faith, it is perhaps particularly obvious in our day and age, when people commit suicide and blow up buildings because of their "faith," that we cannot afford to be gullible, to allow ourselves to be duped and deceived by others or to deceive ourselves.

When the word "faith" appears in the Bible, it means first and foremost *trust* or *confidence in* God, and secondly faithfulness *to* God. Only rarely is the focus on believing the truthfulness of certain propositions. Nevertheless, the question remains on what basis one may accept propositions *about* God, and about religious doctrine more generally. Is it simply a case of blind faith, a leap in the dark? Down the ages most Christians have believed that faith is not something that is opposed to reason, but something that goes beyond it. In other words, there is a place for reason that must be maintained, even if reason alone may not always be sufficient.

Doubt, on the other hand, taken to its extreme, becomes a kind of faith. This may be a surprising idea to some readers, so let me explain what is meant. Extreme unwillingness to believe anything that is not proven can also be viewed as faith that our rational capacities, our senses, our knowledge and understanding are not only adequate, but the only legitimate sources of knowledge. In our time, extreme skepticism might seem altogether appropriate and justified. Where once it could be said that "seeing is believing," today even seeing is not enough. With technology that any young person or teenager can master without much difficulty (and which of course many adults know how to use as well), one can create, manipulate and transform photos so that one is shown meeting famous people, or visiting places one has never been. Although this might seem to be an argument against credulity, and it is, it is also an argument against excessive skepticism. Very soon, technology may blur the lines between the real and the simulated even further, so that it becomes difficult or even impossible to distinguish between the two. This scenario has been explored by philosophers down the ages, and more recently in films such as *The Matrix*, *eXisTenZ* and *The Thirteenth Floor*. The dilemma is whether we can ever be absolutely certain that we are *not* in something like a "matrix," a simulated world that keeps us enslaved. The reality or otherwise of the world we live in appears to be a crucial question, and yet we may not be able to ascertain the answer in a way that would satisfy a skeptic, or at least in a way that would persuade someone who was already utterly convinced that our world *is* in fact a computer simulation. Yet neither can we prove the reverse to be true, namely that this *is* a simulated reality. There are many questions that we cannot answer with absolute certainty, and yet we find ourselves willing to accept some things in the absence of absolute proof. Most of us consider this world that we inhabit to be real. Sometimes, we must take reason as far as it can take us, and then keep moving forward beyond what we can prove.

This book will argue that Christians should, indeed must, discuss questions of *history* in the same way. Historical study deals with evidence, with the question of what we can know about the past, and with what degree of certainty. Christians cannot afford to ignore or bypass such historical investigations. And yet many of Christianity's traditional claims, including (but not limited to) the resurrection of Jesus, may not be able to be proven with certainty, "beyond reasonable doubt," from our perspective in time and space. Of course, some do indeed claim that the resurrection can indeed be proven "beyond doubt," but these claims are usually made by people who are ignoring both the methods of historical study and at least some of the information in the Bible itself. On the pages that follow, we will try to take historical study, rational investigation, as far as it will go. Once we get as far as it can take us, we will ask whether the road necessarily ends there, or whether, having reached the end of our historical investigation, we can carry on, and if so by what means.

Chapter 2
Beyond Reasonable Doubt: How History Works

Past Tense and Present Tension

Historical study asks questions in the past tense – for example, the question "Who was Jesus of Nazareth?" Many today quite naturally and instinctively ask questions about Jesus in the *present* tense – "Who *is* Jesus?" – precisely because Jesus is not simply a figure of the past for them, but a present reality in their experience, or at the very least the object of their reverence. *This* Jesus, the Jesus who is spoken of as a present reality by Christians, is not the one that historians study, nor indeed is this something historians *can* study. The tools of historical inquiry are not designed for such purposes. This is not to say that speaking of Jesus in the present tense is inappropriate, just that in doing so, one refers to Jesus and makes claims about him which are not susceptible to historical scrutiny.

Yet inasmuch as Christians claim that the person they follow in the present is in some sense the *same person* as Jesus of Nazareth who lived in the first century of our era, the results of historical study of that person, of what Christians sometimes refer to as the "earthly life of Jesus," are relevant, indeed crucial. For there is always the tendency to project onto Jesus our own ideals, our own points of view, and to make him in our own image, as it were. If Jesus is viewed as a present reality accessible only to mystics, no claim about him can be substantiated or regarded as secure. One could, in theory, claim anything one wished about Jesus (just as people are prone to do about God more generally). Christians, however, claim that the person who is the focus of their devotion is the same person who lived roughly 2,000 years ago and who can be studied by historians. This historical grounding has the potential to prevent Christianity from simply becoming whatever each individual wishes to make of it. Historical study is a check on our tendency to project onto Jesus that which we want him to be, and to remove from him that which we find unacceptable. As such, not only is the historical study of Jesus not something to be regarded as threatening to Christianity, it is absolutely crucial to it. If Christianity relinquishes its connection to history, all that is left are narratives, stories that may be of the highest value as stories, and may offer deep insights into the human condition, but which may have nothing to do with events that actually happened. Some do indeed consider this to be the appropriate way to approach Christianity: to ignore questions of history and read the Bible symbolically and metaphorically. There is no doubt that the Bible can be approached in this way, and that it can be highly meaningful to do so. However, this does not negate the appropriateness of asking whether the historical figure of Jesus bears any resemblance to the Christ who is the object of Christian faith. If one wishes to worship a Jesus who has no connection to history and historical evidence, one is free to do so – but is it not important that one at least be aware that that is in fact what one is doing?

History and faith

The relationship between history and faith is a complex one. Because *faith* is defined by many people today as believing something without evidence, or even in *spite* of evidence to the contrary, it is no wonder that many view historical study (which is above all a quest for evidence) as at best in tension with faith, and at worst incompatible with it. This definition of faith, however, while a valid meaning of the word in modern English, does not accurately reflect the central and predominant meaning of the words in Hebrew and Greek that are translated as "faith" in the Bible. The Biblical terminology has first and foremost to do with *trust*, with *faithfulness*. It is used most frequently to refer to believing *in* someone (in the Bible it is of course *God* who is the object par excellence of faith, of trust). Faith in the sense of belief *that* certain things are true is of secondary importance, both as a connotation of the word, and in terms of how such belief in the factuality of certain propositions is viewed by Biblical authors. A classic example of this point is James 2:19, which refers to the belief that there is only one God as a correct belief. But according to James, demons also believe that there is only one God. Yet their behavior is not changed in light of such knowledge, and so it is of no benefit to them that they happen to be correct about this point of doctrine. Such knowledge, James asserts, does not bring salvation. The sort of saving faith that Paul talks about so frequently in his letters is confidence in God, which may be supported by beliefs *about* God and God's character, but which are not simply those beliefs.

The Bible also challenges those who believe in God to be open to new information, to new experiences, even though such new data may require that one revise one's theology and indeed one's whole worldview. The classic example is the story of Job, who before his experiences presumably shared his friends' view that God rewards the righteous and punishes the wicked in a fair and consistent manner. Since God is all-powerful and just, how could this not be so? It seems like simple logic. Yet Job's experience showed him that this view of God and of righteousness was too narrow, too simplistic. In a similar way, Paul in his letter to the Galatians argued that the experiences of Gentile converts to Christianity were proof that God had welcomed them into his people, accepting them as they were, even though they had not been circumcised and did not obey the details of the Jewish law. Paul's logic in Galatians 3:4-5 is remarkable, especially when we are aware that Paul had a background in a particular form of Judaism that sought to observe the law strictly and carefully. Since God had poured out his Spirit upon these Gentiles without circumcision, it was clear to Paul that circumcision was no longer a requirement for entry into God's people, no longer a boundary marker delineating who was in and who was out. Paul follows his line of reasoning through to the end and concludes that God must indeed have set aside his earlier covenant in order to make it possible for Gentiles to enter the chosen people. Of course, he does in the end reinterpret Scripture in ways that support his argument, but the fact remains that Paul's new experiences and those of his Gentile converts to Christianity overruled Scripture, at least on this occasion, and led Paul to draw conclusions that he would never have drawn without these experiences.

Although thus far I have been talking about data from *experience* rather than from *historical evidence*, the main reason is that historical study in the modern sense did not exist in Paul's time. To the extent that it did, however, research and fact-finding were considered relevant to faith and not in contradiction to it. See, for example, Luke's description of his research in writing his two-volume work, the Gospel of Luke and the Acts of the Apostles (Luke 1:1-4). Of course, as we shall see later, Luke's own work was concerned not only to accurately gather and record information, but to use that information as a way of teaching something about Christianity. Luke's way of approaching his task is one that can serve as a useful model even today. Faith may go *beyond* historical data, but it should never either *ignore* such information or be in *contradiction* to it. The same goes for data from the sciences as well. The perspective of faith or theology is not the same as a historical or scientific perspective, but as an integrative perspective, it must incorporate data from other levels of understanding and other modes of inquiry, or at the very least be compatible with them.

By way of analogy, we may consider the experience of listening to a piece of music. The enjoyment of listening to the music is not the same as a scientific perspective on the music, which could provide a chemical analysis of the metal from which the violin's strings are made, or which could speak in terms of physics and the frequency of the vibrations in the air when an instrument is played. Yet when I experience the music the instruments produce as *beautiful* and *inspirational*, how does this relate to the scientific perspectives just mentioned? In one sense, it doesn't – it is a completely different level and different perspective on the same objects and the same event. Yet neither is the perspective of the enraptured listener *incompatible* with the data from the sciences. In a similar way, scientific and historical data do not in and of themselves support or invalidate theological claims, but merely provide information that is relevant to the ways in which we think and speak about God. To deny a physical analysis of music on the basis that it does not account for one's being moved by the music is to make a category mistake. These are different ways of analyzing and appreciating the same phenomena.

In the same way, the perspective of faith must *be compatible with* data from history and science, even as it inevitably goes beyond it. Let us consider the famous passage in Hebrews 11:1, which states that "Faith is the assurance of things hoped for, the conviction of things not seen". The emphasis, once again, is on *trusting God* for things that are not seen because they have not yet been brought about. Nonetheless, there is also an emphasis on faith as enabling the believer to feel confident about spiritual things that cannot be seen with the eye or felt with our fingers. Nothing in this passage, however, suggests that faith means, or provides a basis for, either disregarding what is visible or believing things that contradict what we can see. Faith may indeed allow us to go beyond the visible, and thus also beyond the historical and the scientific, but it does not allow us to ignore those sources of information and human knowledge. If faith enables us to view a situation that seems hopeless as not hopeless, it is not because faith allows us to deny the reality of human suffering or whatever else may be leading people to feel despair. Faith may lead us to hope because it trusts that there is more to the situation than meets the eye; but it does not lead us to pretend that those who clearly are suffering are not. Faith may go beyond the available evidence, but if it contradicts it, it is at best wishful thinking and at worst a delusion or a lie.

To revisit the language used in Hebrews 11:1

once more, faith may make it possible for us to feel confident about the reality of what is unseen. But the reverse is not the case: faith does *not* allow us to deny the reality of that which is visible. Returning to the topic we raised earlier, the perspective of faith may wish to say things about Jesus in the present tense. However appropriate this may be, such present-tense statements ought to *at least be compatible with* the historical evidence about Jesus, even though they need not necessarily be *limited to* the historical data. And so from the outset it is important to understand *who* we are studying if we seek to look at Jesus using the tools historians use. We are studying the *historical Jesus*, a figure who lived and died in the ancient world, in the past, and in studying him and drawing conclusions about him *as historians* we must limit ourselves only what we can confirm from historical data.

The aims of a historian may usefully be compared to those of a prosecuting attorney, and indeed we shall explore this analogy further at many points throughout this book. The question of whether someone is guilty or not guilty can rarely if ever be proved or disproved so thoroughly and so convincingly that new evidence could never change things and lead to an appeal and a different verdict. The attorney aims to prove his case either *beyond reasonable doubt*, or *more probable than not*, depending on the type of trial. The lawyer makes his or her case based on the available evidence. The historian has a similar task: to set forth what can be known or hypothesized, and with what degree of certainty, based on whatever evidence there is available that can withstand careful, critical inspection and scrutiny.

Obviously Jesus is more than merely the sum of the information a historian can recover about him, much less the things that a historian can *prove beyond reasonable doubt* concerning him. This is true of *all* historical figures, and Jesus is no exception (see John 20:30 and 21:25, which acknowledge this very point, that there is much more to the story of Jesus than is recorded in that particular book, or indeed than we could ever hope to record in written records). Just imagine that someone in the distant future undertook a historical investigation of *your* life. Even if you yourself had written something (Jesus, as far as we know, did not), even if several biographies were written about you, would those future generations ever fully grasp the "real you"? Would there not always be something missing from any portrait or depiction? The point of historical study is not to provide us with a comprehensive understanding of a historical individual. The point is to provide us with information that is as accurate as possible and as certain as possible, assisting us as we seek to understand as much as we can about particular individuals and events from the past.

Partial Evidence, Partial Sources

Historians have to deal not only with evidence that is *partial* in the sense of *incomplete*, but also with evidence that is *partial* in the sense of *biased*. Indeed, those figures in whom historians (and people in general) tend to be most interested are ones who were controversial in their time, and in many cases they remain controversial long after that. Those who take the time to write about someone usually consider that person important in some way – either because they are felt to be having a positive impact on the world, or because they are viewed as having a negative impact. Regularly one will find different sources that view the same individual in radically different ways, written by his or her supporters and detractors respectively. Bias seems inevitable, and historians are aware of this. As a result, historians treat their sources critically, with an appropriate measure of skepticism. Some historians may be inclined to give their sources the benefit of the doubt, and to assume their accuracy unless they find clear evidence to the contrary. Others will only accept evidence that can be corroborated. These different approaches to sources and evidence will in all likelihood lead to different conclusions. Both have their place, and in seeking to learn about the past it is important to gather as much information and as many different perspectives as possible.

In historical study, as in any field or discipline, the average interested layperson will be at least somewhat dependent on experts, who have studied the primary sources in their original languages, found and/or examined archaeological data, and are knowledgeable about the time period under investigation. Yet when it comes to historical perspectives on Jesus and the Bible, one will at times hear radically contradictory claims being made. How can one evaluate them? The best course of action is the same whether one is seeking expert opinions about history and archaeology, Biblical studies, technical problems with your car or computer, or medical advice and diagnoses. It is always worth getting a second opinion, and perhaps even a third opinion. But it is never a good idea to just look for someone who says what you want to hear. If one reads recent books and articles by several reputable historians (individuals who work at institutions of higher education and have had their work published in journals and other forums that require them to first be reviewed anonymously by peers), irrespective whether the subject is Jesus and early Christianity or something else altogether, one will be able to get a genuine sense of the state of our knowledge. If there is something about which most historians or other experts agree, it will be something that is reasonably certain – not absolutely certain, but as certain as possible based on the evidence available. If there are points of major disagreement, this too is instructive. It means either that we do not have the necessary evidence to be certain about this point, or that the evidence can be interpreted in more than one way, or that there are disagreements about whether certain details in our available sources are accurate. Historical study deals in probabilities rather than absolute certainties – again, just like a court of law. Both the agreements and the disagreements of historians can teach those interested in history something. But one will not get a genuine sense of the results of historical investigation by reading only those books likely to confirm what one already thinks, nor by latching on to and regarding as authoritative only those historians whose conclusions confirm one's presuppositions. If we are to do justice to the available data from the Bible and elsewhere, we must seek to be fair. We play the part of the jury, and we should aim to "give Jesus a fair trial", as it were.

History and Archaeology: Some Persons or Events May Have Been Dramatized

Evidence from archaeology and from other historical sources will at times confirm the accuracy of information provided in the Bible. At other times, it will merely supplement it, providing useful background information that helps us make sense of the stories told therein. But at times, historical evidence will be found that is incompatible with the information in a Biblical text. Such evidence regularly leads historians to conclude that the text in question cannot be considered a straightforward historical account, one that is literally and precisely factual. Unfortunately, many readers of the Bible today assume that they must at all costs regard its stories as precise historical reports, even if it means ignoring clear evidence to the contrary. This is not only a poor course of action that discredits Christianity and suggests that faith and reason are incompatible. It is also unnecessary. Jesus told many parables, and these stories can be insightful, challenging, meaningful and powerful without necessarily being stories about actual events. To focus on proving that there really was a man who walked the road from Jerusalem to Jericho on a given day, was beaten and robbed, and eventually rescued by a Samaritan, would seem to me (and, I would hope, to most Christians) to be entirely missing the point of the story, which is to challenge national, racial and religious prejudice, as well as help us to view our responsibility to others in the broadest possible terms by applying the Golden Rule.

Why is it that so many today assume that most if not all Biblical literature is straightforward factual description, and treat this as the "default setting" when reading the Bible? The Bible in fact seems to contain a much more diverse range of genres, and in order to see this, one only needs to read the stories with an openness to pick up on relevant cues. Might stories that feature talking animals be fables, or at least fable-like? When the opponents in the Gospel of John come across as bumbling idiots, might we not be dealing with parody or caricature? Anyone who has read the Gospels carefully will be aware that these authors were not primarily concerned with matters that are paramount to modern historians – for instance, chronology. The Gospel authors clearly take the stories and sayings about Jesus they are recording and arrange them so as to make a theological point, or to make their Gospel useful for teaching purposes. There are a wider range of options than simply "inerrantly-recorded history" on the one end and "pure fiction" on the other. If the Gospels were made into movies in our time, would they bear the disclaimer at the end that "some persons or events may have been dramatized"? And if they did, might modern readers be better prepared for the possibility that what one finds in the Gospels is neither pure fact nor pure fiction, but something in between?

As a rule, in a historical investigation archaeological evidence trumps textual evidence, since artifacts take us directly to a given time and place, whereas any written accounts will by definition be later, sometimes significantly later. Furthermore, the stories people tell are not always accurate, even when they are aiming to be, and memory has been demonstrated time and again to be prone to errors and delusions. Moreover, not everyone who tells a story is in fact *intending* to provide accurate information, and when one is dealing with stories transmitted orally over several decades, the possibility for growth, omission and misunderstanding obviously exists. Once again, when considering the relationship between textual and archaeological evidence, we may draw a close parallel to criminal investigations. Ideally, a prosecutor wants there to be *both* physical evidence *and* testimony, and for both to agree. However, if evidence from forensics and ballistics contradicts someone's testimony, the hard evidence will be given priority. The same applies to historical study, including in relation to events recounted in the Bible.

On the other hand, archaeological evidence must itself be investigated, just as the physical evidence in a criminal case must be. Has the evidence been tampered with or contaminated? Could the evidence be compatible with more than one conclusion? In the realm of Biblical archaeology, there have been many fraudulent claims (among the most famous are the claims to have found chariot wheels in the Red Sea, and the multiple claims to have discovered Noah's Ark), and there are still others where the authenticity of the artifacts or inscriptions is in doubt. Where there is uncertainty, it is often because the artifacts have been recovered by "tomb raiders" rather than archaeologists, so that the archaeological context of the find is obscured or lost altogether. However, in the case of the Talpiot tomb, which contains ossuaries inscribed with names like "Jesus son of Joseph" and "Mary," the tomb was investigated and its contents recorded by official archaeologists, and so there is no doubt about the authenticity of the tomb or of the ossuaries found therein. What is in doubt is whether the "Josh son of Joe" whose bones once resided in the tomb was Jesus of Nazareth. *If* the tomb can be shown to belong to this particular Jesus son of Joseph who is central to Christianity, then this evidence will have to take priority over textual accounts, however uncomfortable the consequences. However, because names like Jesus/Joshua, Joseph and Mary were extremely common in this period (the latter being estimated as the name borne by fully one quarter of all Jewish women in the time of Jesus), this is a "big if."

Speaking of Trust…

Having emphasized earlier the idea of faith as *trust*, it may seem odd to some that this book is not encouraging readers of the New Testament to *trust* those texts. However, according to precisely those very same New Testament writings, the appropriate object of faith is not a set of writings but *God*. Indeed, from a theological perspective, the emphasis in some streams of contemporary Christianity on placing one's trust in a book and regarding it as inerrant is a form of *idolatry*. Idolatry, the prohibition of which is listed high among the Ten Commandments, initially referred to the literal making of statues and "graven images," but there is a long history of expanding the concept to cover any transfer to created things of prerogatives and attributes appropriately belonging to God alone. That many modern Christians treat the Bible in an idolatrous way when the Bible itself contains so many warnings about idolatry is painfully ironic.

But it is not for *theological* reasons that *historians* cannot simply trust texts. The writing of the first of the New Testament Gospels is generally thought to have taken place some three or four decades after the crucifixion. Roughly the same amount of time has passed between the assassination of John F. Kennedy and the time this book was first published. There are numerous books and movies on the latter subject, and there are both official and conspiracy-theory accounts of what actually happened. Could someone 2,000 years from now simply read some of the texts being written today and assume (or "trust") that they accurately depict the events in question, that they tell "what really happened"? Imagine if we lived in a world without videotape, without newspapers, how much less certainty we would have about these events even from our own standpoint in history. Consider how much more difficult it would be under those circumstances to gather any information at all, much less information that is accurate and can be confirmed with a high degree of probability. The parallels are not intended to be precise, but merely illustrative: there can be texts that accurately reflect events, ones that reinterpret what happened, and even ones that seek to obscure what really happened. A historian may, having found corroborating evidence for most of the claims made in a particular text, be more inclined to trust those details that lack corroborating evidence. But a historian can never simply trust a text without first engaging in the painstaking task of assessing the reliability of the testimony it contains, and looking to see what details are confirmed or denied in other sources.

Claims of Biblical inerrancy, and sometimes even more modest claims of Biblical accuracy, are often coupled with dismissal of the results of historical and scientific investigations. This approach will not persuade anyone who takes even a moment to think about the subject. To claim that the Bible is inerrant, and then to explain away or refuse to acknowledge evidence to the contrary, is similar to the famous sign found in workplaces, offering two rules: (1) The Bible is always right, and (2) If the Bible is wrong, see rule number one. This is circular reasoning at its worst. It is only by means of historical investigation that we can assess the historicity of Biblical stories. To claim that the Bible is inerrant, and to refuse to pay attention to the results of the one discipline that can assess such claims, namely historical study, is the equivalent of maintaining that one is healthy regardless of one's symptoms and while refusing to be examined by a doctor. To approach the Bible in this way is not simply misguided, it is downright dishonest.

As a Christian, I strongly dislike having to emphasize points such as these, since to some readers it will seem that I am leading people to take a negative view of the Bible. That is not my aim. One of my aims *is* to help those who adopt a position on either extreme, claiming that the Biblical literature is entirely accurate or entirely inaccurate, to understand that *neither* extreme viewpoint is justified by historical study. The evidence suggests that Biblical accounts of historical events for the most part lie somewhere in between the extremes, at various points along the spectrum, and many contain at least some reliable information that historians can use. An all-or-nothing approach is in fact antithetical to and incompatible with the methods of historical study. Each piece of evidence must be examined. For example, from a historian's perspective, the Gospel of Mark (usually considered the earliest of the four canonical Gospels) is assessed as being on the whole more reliable than the Gospel of John (in which Jesus, John the Baptist, and the narrator all speak in the same style and vocabulary, as can be seen particularly clearly in chapter 3 of that Gospel). Yet there will be details in each that are evaluated as being accurate, while others are deemed to be historically unlikely. A historian must investigate each document, and each detail in a given document, on its own merits.

Some will surely object that this is submitting the Bible to human judgment as a higher authority. That is certainly correct – and, I would ask, how could it be otherwise? Even those who claim to "believe the whole Bible" and to "take the Bible literally" do not really do either of these things. In actual fact, they ignore whole huge segments of the Bible that do not suit their interests, they interpret as metaphorical anything that clearly cannot be taken literally (e.g. the dome over the earth that holds up the waters above mentioned in Genesis 1:6) while at the same time arguing with or condemning anyone who interprets other details in the same way, and all the while claiming they are taking the *whole* Bible literally. Such an approach not only is *not* based on the authority of Scripture, it utterly disrespects the Bible, and ignores that the interpretative frameworks being used to make sense of the Bible – such as inerrancy and so-called literalism – are equally human judgments. In reality, it is the person who approaches the Bible historically, who is willing to take the time and effort to evaluate each claim and each affirmation, that is treating the Bible with the seriousness and respect it deserves. When reading the Bible, one always already has in place a set of assumptions about what the Bible is and how to interpret it. Historical study provides a set of tools that allow one to be as fair and impartial in evaluating the evidence as is humanly possible. This obviously doesn't mean that historians are not influenced by their presuppositions and their own limited point of view. What it does mean is that historical study provides a way for evaluating not only the relevant data, but also the arguments made by other historians, and to realize when a piece of evidence is not being given a "fair trial."

Who Wrote the Gospels?

Particularly if we had lived in a time in which written sources were less common, but even in our own context today, if we wanted to investigate an event in the past, we would presumably seek out eyewitness testimony wherever possible. This raises the question of whether the New Testament sources provide us with such eyewitness testimony. Although there are ongoing debates about this subject, most historians and Biblical scholars conclude that the New Testament Gospels do not give us *direct access* to *firsthand accounts* of eyewitness testimony. Many readers of the Bible are unaware that the titles given to these books are not part of the books themselves and are not found in our earliest manuscripts. Such information is readily available in academic study Bibles and in commentaries, but such sources are often neglected, even by those who claim that the Bible is important to them. Once one becomes aware that these texts were written anonymously, that the texts themselves in their earliest form do not attribute authorship to named individuals, then one clearly can no longer assume that the information provided in them represents eyewitness testimony, much less that it is *reliable* eyewitness testimony. Each text must be evaluated in terms of its content, and if one wishes to discuss matters of authorship, one must assess the reliability of those church traditions which attribute these Gospels to Matthew, Mark, Luke and John.

The Gospel of Mark is usually dated earliest (for reasons we shall explain in the next section), and the early church tradition that an individual named Mark was the author is plausible, precisely because that individual was neither one of the twelve apostles nor an eyewitness. The early Church is therefore unlikely to have simply made this up. Whenever possible, the Church attributed writings to apostolic sources and eyewitnesses – a quick glance at the names of the purported authors of the later extracanonical Gospels will confirm this. Matthew's Gospel may in fact be one of our earliest instances of just such an attribution to an apostle for this reason. It is, at the very least, unlikely to have been written by the apostle and former tax collector. The reason for attributing it specifically to Matthew is probably because this Gospel calls an individual "Matthew" where the other Gospels in the same story call him "Levi" (Matthew 9:9; compare Mark 2:14). But this passage also provides strong evidence against Matthew having been the author. It is highly unlikely that Matthew, writing a Gospel of his own, would tell of his first encounter with Jesus in words taken entirely from Mark's Gospel.

The Gospel of Luke, like the Gospel of Mark, may well stem from its traditionally purported author, since Luke too was not an eyewitness of the events he describes, and there is no obvious reason the early church would have invented such an attribution. Finally, the Gospel of John probably does not stem from John the son of Zebedee, one of the twelve. It seems to derive from the testimony of a Judean disciple of Jesus, and based on internal evidence, the "disciple whom Jesus loved," described in John 21:24 as the one who testified to the things written in the Gospel, would more readily be identified with Lazarus of Bethany (see John 11:3, where he is referred to as the one Jesus loves). However, from a historical perspective, it is not only the identity of this disciple that is uncertain, but whether he should be understood as a real person or an ideal type, since he is inserted into the story in John in places where other Gospels not only fail to mention him, but seem to presuppose that none of Jesus' male disciples was present. At any rate, clearly whoever put the Gospel in its present form and wrote about the testimony of the "beloved disciple" in the third person (in chapter 21) was someone other than the beloved disciple, and thus here too we have, at best, eyewitness testimony once removed. Nevertheless, for convenience, as is the usual practice in Biblical studies, I shall continue to use the traditional names for the Gospels and their authors, since the alternative is to refer on each occasion to "the author of the Gospel of Mark" or "the author of the Gospel traditionally attributed to Matthew", which is far too cumbersome. But in doing so, it must be clear that I am not assuming that the authors of these texts are eyewitnesses, much less members of Jesus' inner circle of followers.

Testimony about what someone claims to have heard from an eyewitness would not stand up in a court of law today – it is what is known as "hearsay". Nevertheless, sometimes hearsay is all a historian has, and the rules of historical investigation are not as strict as those of the American legal system. We can utilize any sources available, and the only consequence will be that our conclusions about what happened will be less certain than if we had first-hand accounts written by the eyewitnesses themselves. However, serious difficulties arise when we are uncertain how many steps removed from the eyewitnesses we happen to be. We may mention as an example Paul's reference in 1 Corinthians 15:6 to the risen Jesus having appeared to 500 people at one time. This sounds like impressive evidence for the resurrection, and it is a popular verse for apologists to cite. Yet it is clear that Paul was not himself one of those 500 (since he relates his own first encounter with Jesus after that, in verse 8), and we do not know whether Paul heard this story directly from someone who was one of those five hundred individuals allegedly present on that occasion. Nor can we ascertain whether all of those present on that occasion, if there was indeed such an occasion, were all in agreement regarding the nature of the experience they had, much less about what if anything it might prove. And so we find ourselves in a situation in which we can only wonder what happened if anything, who told the story, whether the number grew with the retelling, and so on. One need only investigate modern claims of miracles – whether circulated orally or via e-mail – to see how such stories can develop and grow, as well as the difficulty in ascertaining who first told them and the extent to which they reflect actual events. The question of authorship is thus an important one for a historian, and our information about the authorship of the Gospels does not allow us to simply treat them as first-hand testimony, which might have inclined us to give them "the benefit of the doubt". Rather, each detail, each claim, each story and each saying must be considered on its own merits, and compared with other evidence, before drawing a conclusion.

In such cases, having multiple independent sources providing the same information can make up for our lack of first-hand accounts. And so it is that we must now consider the relationship between the Gospels, and whether in those instances in which we have the same story in more than one Gospel, we have *independent* testimony to the same event, or whether it is more likely that one or more of the Gospel authors has derived his information from another Gospel or some other earlier written source.

The Synoptic Problem

At this point we must discuss the topic of the interrelationship between the Gospels of Matthew, Mark and Luke, which are often referred to as the "Synoptic Gospels" because the traditional name for a book that presents all three in parallel columns is a *synopsis* of the Gospels. The Greek word from which *synoptic* derives means "seeing together," and that too appropriately reflects their similar content. These three Gospels overlap substantially, and the question of how to account for the interrelationship is known as the "Synoptic Problem," which is just shorthand for "the problem of figuring out the relationship between the Gospels of Matthew, Mark and Luke."

There is a general consensus among Biblical scholars that Mark's Gospel was the first of the New Testament Gospels to be written. At those points at which they have material in common with Mark's Gospel, both Matthew and Luke generally follow Mark's order. If Matthew departs from Mark's order, generally Luke doesn't follow him, and likewise when Luke departs from Mark's order, Matthew generally doesn't follow him. This seems to suggest that both Luke and Matthew used Mark's Gospel independently of one another in writing their own Gospels, and that Mark's Gospel is the earliest Gospel we have in the New Testament canon. The fact that they agree not only on the wording of sayings of Jesus and stories about him, but also on the *order* in which the stories and sayings are strung together, indicates that they knew these stories arranged in Mark's Gospel and not merely through verbal contact with the oral traditions of early Christianity. Finally, the fact that Matthew and Luke do not tend to follow one another when they depart from Mark's order suggests that Matthew and Luke each used Mark's Gospel independently of one another.

There is further evidence in the details of the stories where Mark and other Gospels overlap, indicating that Mark indeed came first. Compare the accounts of the execution of John the Baptist in Mark 6:16-29 and Matthew 14:1-12. Even reading in English translation, it is easy to see how the story not only follows the same basic outline, but overlaps word for word in places. You will also see how, in editing the material he took over from Mark, Matthew has introduced a tension into the story. Whereas Mark's account is consistent in presenting Herod as sympathetic to John, Matthew introduces early on the idea that Herod wanted to kill him (Matthew 14:5, in contrast to Mark 6:19-20), so that when he later includes Mark's statement that Herod was grieved to find himself bound by a promise to kill John (Matthew 14:9), the reader is left wondering why. The best explanation is that Matthew was copying from Mark's Gospel, and followed Mark at this point, without noticing the tension with what he himself had written earlier, in crafting his own version of the story.

Another clear sign that the dependence is literary (and not simply dependence on the same oral tradition) can be seen if we compare Matthew 24:15-16 with its source, Mark 13:14:

Mark 13:14	Matthew 24:15-16
But *when you see the desolating sacrilege*	So *when you see the desolating sacrilege*
set up where it ought not to be	standing in the holy place, as was spoken of by the prophet Daniel
(let the reader understand),	**(let the reader understand)**,
then those in Judea must flee to the mountains…	*then those in Judea must flee to the mountains…*

Here too there are significant word-for-word agreements between Mark and Matthew, while the points at which Matthew differs from Mark clearly represent Matthew seeking to clarify, interpret, and elaborate on what Mark wrote, in this case explaining that the "desolating sacrilege" is something spoken of in the book of Daniel, and that the place it ought not to be is the holy place, i.e. the Temple. But the clearest indication of a *literary* dependence between these two Gospels is found in the words "let the reader understand" (in bold above). This parenthetical remark is clearly an addition by Mark, since it calls for the *reader* of the Gospel to understand (in contrast to the language Jesus himself is said to have used in addressing his audiences verbally, "whoever has ears to hear, let them hear", or as we might put it today, "If you've got ears, use 'em"). Matthew does not simply reproduce the same oral tradition as Mark, but also reproduces Mark's editorial comments, and so it is clear that he knows the Gospel of Mark as a *written* source.

Yet Matthew does not always reproduce Mark's editorial comments and parenthetical remarks, presumably because he didn't entirely agree with them. It is also likely that, even though Matthew clearly used Mark, he may also have known some of the same material from oral tradition as well, so that at times he was able to distinguish between tradition and redaction (that is, editorial comments) in what Mark wrote. A good example is found in Mark 7:18-20 and its parallel in Matthew 15:17-18:

Mark 7:18-20	Matthew 15:17-18
…Do you not see that whatever goes into a person from outside cannot defile, since it enters, not the heart but the stomach, and goes out into the sewer?'	Do you not see that whatever goes into the mouth enters the stomach, and goes out into the sewer?
(Thus he declared all foods clean.)	
And he said, 'It is what comes out of a person that defiles.	But what comes out of the mouth proceeds from the heart, and this is what defiles.

It is easy to see how Mark's wording, which is perhaps intentionally vague, is clarified and explained in Matthew's Gospel, which specifies that the reason food cannot truly defile a person is that it enters the stomach and not the heart. This tendency to explain, to clarify, and to tie up loose ends is a characteristic trait of Matthew's Gospel. But note the parenthetical comment by Mark (once again in bold), which is clearly an editorial remark, since it is not Jesus speaking at that point. What is striking is that this time, although

Matthew is seeking to reproduce and at the same time to clarify the teaching of Jesus preserved in Mark 7, he omits Mark's own clarification/interpretation of Jesus' words. They were perhaps a bit too like Paul's teaching for Matthew, who emphasizes the ongoing value and validity of the Law of Moses, in contrast with Paul's emphasis on Gentile Christians not needing to convert to Judaism and observe the details of the Mosaic Law in order to become Christians. At any rate, here we see that, although Matthew used Mark's Gospel as a source, he does not always reproduce Mark's parenthetical and interpretative asides. This might represent Matthew's *editing* of Mark, and it clearly *is* that. But in some instances it may also indicate that Matthew knew stories about Jesus and sayings attributed to him *independently* of Mark as well. In such cases, rather than understanding himself to be changing a story about something Jesus said or did, he may instead have understood himself to be reverting the story or saying to the form in which he had always heard it.

Matthew's use of Mark in the manner we have outlined here thus seems likely. But we also find that there are overlaps between Matthew and Luke where there is no parallel in Mark. One way to explain this would be to suggest that either Matthew used Luke or Luke used Matthew. Yet both Matthew and Luke, in using Mark, took over most of what Mark wrote and incorporated it into their own Gospels. If one does not posit the literary dependence of Matthew upon Luke or vice versa, then how can one account for the points of intersection and overlap between them on details which are not in Mark's Gospel? On the other hand, if Matthew knew Luke's Gospel of vice versa, why do they omit so much of each other's material, and diverge so drastically even at those points where they do overlap somewhat, and why do they do so without offering any explanation?

In order to solve this problem, scholars have proposed the existence of an earlier source other than Mark, which was used by both Matthew and Luke independently of one another, and which consisted primarily of sayings of Jesus. In the prologue to his Gospel, Luke refers to "many" who have undertaken to write about Jesus prior to himself, and so it should not surprise us to find that there were other written accounts of what Jesus said and did. Perhaps one reason this source was not preserved is precisely because most or all of it was now available in Matthew and Luke. To make it easy to refer to, this common source for the non-Markan material that Matthew and Luke share is designated with the abbreviation "Q.".

In order to see the evidence for this common source, one needs only look at the relationship between Matthew's "Sermon on the Mount" and Luke's "Sermon on the Plain". If readers take two Bibles and place them side by side, they will easily be able to see how material in Luke chapter 6 not only appears in Matthew chapters 5-7, but appears there in essentially the same order, albeit with Matthew having inserted other sayings of Jesus in places that relate to the same theme or topic. Below we provide some of the key points of overlap and their common order in both Gospels:

	Luke 6	Matthew 5-7
Beatitudes	20b-23	5:3-12
Love of enemy	27-36	5:38-47
Do not judge	37-38	7:1-2
Splinter and beam	41-42	7:3-5
Tree and fruit	43-45	7:16-20
Lord, Lord	46	7:21
Comparing houses	47-49	7:24-27

As can be seen from a comparison of these two passages, both Matthew and Luke have added to what they found in their source, "Q". Matthew has a tendency to organize teaching into large sections by topic, as is clearly the case in the "Sermon on the Mount." It is obviously far more likely that Matthew organized Jesus' teaching thematically into a single discourse, than that Luke found something like the Sermon on the Mount in his source and decided to take the material from it and scatter it seemingly at random throughout his Gospel. For this reason, Luke is generally thought to more accurately preserve the order of "Q," although not always the exact wording and content, when compared with Matthew. At any rate, it can be seen that in this passage, although both supplement their common source, both Matthew and Luke for the most part follow its order. One significant change is the "Golden Rule," which both include, but which Matthew moves so as to place it at a more climactic moment. Luke 11:1-13 provides other material that in Matthew's Gospel is included in the "Sermon on the Mount", most notably a shorter version of the Lord's Prayer.

Perhaps the clearest evidence that Matthew did not use Luke, nor Luke Matthew, is the fact that they contain two contradictory genealogies (Matthew 1:1-16; Luke 3:23-38). Even if one comes up with a plausible reason why one would have "corrected" the genealogy of the other, if they had done so we might have expected them to at least explain *why* the change was being made. The best explanation is therefore that neither had access to the other's Gospel, and likewise neither had the genealogical information that the other had. The genealogies of Luke and Matthew are a genuine historical difficulty, since both authors claim to be providing genealogies of Joseph, contrary to the common assertion (even made in the documentary about the Talpiot tomb) that the one in Luke is *Mary's* genealogy (Luke 3:23 explicitly states that this too is supposed to be Joseph's genealogy). There have been numerous attempts to force them to agree, but these so-called "solutions" do far less justice to what these texts actually say than does the admission that we have an irreconcilable contradiction. There is no way of knowing whether either of them actually had access to authentic genealogical information from Jesus' family. And so, not only can they not both be correct, but we have no way of knowing whether *either* is correct.

The points we have made thus far hopefully establish the independence of the Gospels of Matthew and Luke from one another. But what then are we to make of the few places where Matthew and Luke agree against Mark? In some cases, this may be explained as being due to Mark and Q having overlapped. One example of this is the story of Jesus' temptation in the wilderness, which Mark mentions briefly but which Matthew and Luke clearly know from another, common source. In other cases there is no need to posit an overlap between Mark and Q: it is plausible that Matthew and Luke made similar improvements to Mark's grammar or to other aspects of his narrative. Mark's Greek and his style are often "unpolished," and it is not surprising that, in changing what Mark wrote to better Greek, both Matthew and Luke would make the same or at least very similar changes. In still other cases theological motives can explain their editing of Mark in much the same way. A good example of this is found in Mark 12:8 and parallels. You will notice if you look at Matthew 21:39 and Luke 20:15 that both Matthew and Luke change the order of events found in Mark, to one that is far less obvious and logical than that found in Mark. How is this to be explained? Presumably both Matthew and Luke regarded the parable of the tenants as an allegory of Jesus' rejection and execution in Jerusalem, and therefore they changed the order to fit the fact that Jesus was first taken outside the city (represented in the parable by the vineyard) and then killed. Here, we can see how concern to make earlier sayings and traditions more accurately "fit the facts" of what actually happened could lead both Matthew and Luke to make similar changes to Mark, one of the two sources they both used.

A good passage to refer to in concluding our discussion of Matthew's use of sources is Matthew 16:13-20. There, Matthew adds words praising Peter for his confession, which are not found in either Mark or Luke. Is it likely that either Mark or Luke, had they known Matthew's version, would have changed it in such a way as to almost call into question the validity of Peter's confession of Jesus as the Anointed One? Here once again we see that the most logical explanation is that Matthew used Mark, and that the material Matthew and Luke have in common is to be explained in terms of a common source rather than in terms of a literary interdependence between them. And thus we conclude that the "two source" explanation of the Synoptic problem (i.e. that Matthew and Luke each used Mark and "Q" independently of one another) is the most convincing explanation of the phenomena found in these Gospels. This explanation can be outlined as follows:

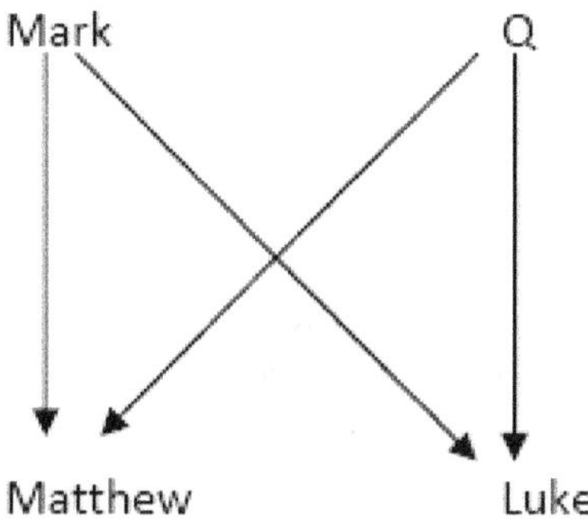

Whether Matthew and Luke used other written sources is less clear, though Luke certainly is intriguing in his reference to *many* having previously undertaken to write about these things. In the end, we are left with two clearly independent early sources, namely Mark and "Q," and it is to these, together with the letters of Paul, that historians turn first in searching for the most reliable information they can obtain about the historical figure of Jesus. The reason for preferring earlier sources is obvious: they bring us the closest to the actual time in which Jesus said what he said and did what he did.

Witnesses and collusion

Understanding the relationship between the Gospels is crucial for historians, because historians do not simply look for sources that agree, but ones that agree *independently* of one another. Returning to the analogy with a criminal investigation, it is one thing to have two witnesses tell essentially the same story, and another thing altogether to have two witnesses tell the *exact same story* in the *exact same words*. In the latter case, rather than this agreement strengthening their testimony, it will undermine it altogether, because it is apparent that the witnesses conferred with one another and rehearsed a common story. This is not to suggest, of course, that the Gospel authors conferred with one another in precisely this way. The Gospels of Matthew and Luke used Mark as a source, and at times they edit their source material. They did not confer with one another as authors and agree to write the same things: had they done so, we would expect them to agree even more often than they actually do. The point of the illustration is simply that, if Matthew and Luke agree with Mark because they read Mark and reproduced stories from his Gospel by copying them, then they do not provide independent attestation to that story. Instead of having three witnesses to particular events in such cases, we have only *one*, with two other individuals having heard this person's testimony and repeated it themselves. And in each case, even our earliest sources (Mark and "Q") do not clearly bring us back into direct contact with an eyewitness. We thus have to take into account a period of memory and oral transmission, during which stories about Jesus and sayings attributed to him were passed on by word of mouth.

Retelling Stories

In seeking to understand the ways in which early Christians passed on traditions about Jesus by word of mouth, Biblical scholars have at times appealed to insights from experts working in other fields, such as the study of folklore or the epics retold in story and song within oral cultures. Yet the truth is that the period of oral transmission we are dealing with in the case of the sayings of and stories about Jesus is much shorter than in these other instances. Probably some thirty years or so passed, in the estimation of most historians, between the events of the life of the historical Jesus and their first being recorded in writing. During at least most of this period, there were still individuals involved in the early Christian church who had actually witnessed the public ministry of Jesus. Of course, we do not know whether such eyewitnesses were in close geographic proximity to the authors of the Gospels. If Mark wrote in Rome (as church tradition in fact suggests), but Peter, instead of having been present there with Mark, was in Jerusalem, would the fact that Peter was an eyewitness and still alive in any way ensure the accuracy of what Mark wrote? In fact, in spite of the church tradition to that effect, we do not know whether Mark actually heard Peter tell the stories included in his Gospel at all. More likely is that early eyewitnesses told stories and passed on teachings as they planted churches. This information was preserved, but also expanded and reinterpreted, within that Christian community, as it was applied to the needs and situations of Christian believers. In some cases, words spoken by Christian prophets in the name of the risen Jesus may have been included as sayings of Jesus. In other cases, recommendations made and sermon illustrations used by church leaders may have been mistakenly attributed to Jesus. In fact, in the writings of Christian leaders after the New Testament period, we occasionally find just that: well-known proverbs and other such sayings are mistakenly attributed to Jesus. And anyone who has ever tried to stop a rumor they knew to be untrue will be aware that the existence of eyewitnesses doesn't always prevent other versions being told, spreading, and even predominating.

Sayings were passed on by means of a vibrant oral tradition, in which one would expect to find the gist of stories and sayings preserved and passed on, but also adaptation and development of the material in the process. It was not the case during this early period that the sayings of Jesus existed in writing, there to be memorized word for word, with a written original against which one could check the precise wording while seeking to memorize them. When dealing with oral tradition, the whole notion of something being preserved "word for word" does not exist in the same way that it does in highly literate societies. A *word* in such a context is not a series of letters but a sound that is experienced as a transitory event conveying an idea or impression. What was involved in the transmission and preservation of information in a primarily oral context is hard for most of us to imagine. Since we see changes being made to written accounts by those who used them in writing their own Gospels at a later time, how can we possibly imagine that it was any different in the period before there were written accounts?

As stories were retold in and applied to new contexts, they were often shaped by that process, and sometimes the use to which a saying or story was put in between its first telling and its being written down has left its mark on some of the details. Thus there are different levels to the stories incorporated in the Synoptic Gospels:

(1) There is the teaching of Jesus
(2) which was retold and passed on orally (and/or in written form) in the church before
(3) being placed in the written form accessible to us by the authors of the Gospels.

We need to keep these different levels in mind if we want to understand the Gospels. Similarly, in every story there are two levels that we may relate to, one or both of which may have influenced the present form of the narrative in important ways:

(1) The historical level, in which Jesus said or did such and such, and
(2) the contextual level, in which the Gospel writer (or someone at an earlier time) applied this tradition about Jesus to needs and situations in their own time and church.

These correspond at least in part to the two major different approaches to the Gospels that one may adopt: historical and literary. In essence, a historian is not interested in the story that is told in a written text for its own sake. The historian is interested in getting back *behind* the text, using the text as a means of gaining access to events that supposedly happened earlier. A literary approach, on the other hand, reads the text at face value, and may tell us what a particular author appears to have been concerned to emphasize, or what the character of Simon Peter is like in one of the Gospels. A literary approach, however, cannot answer the question of whether the portrait of Simon Peter as a character in a particular book reflects the personality and characteristics of an actual person by that name. To answer those sorts of questions, one needs to use the tools of historical study. In a nutshell, both these approaches are useful, but they are useful for answering different sorts of question. A literary approach enables one to grasp the meaning of a story on the level of the text itself. A historical approach digs through and seeks to get behind a text to see what if anything can be determined about actual historical events. This may be illustrated as follows:

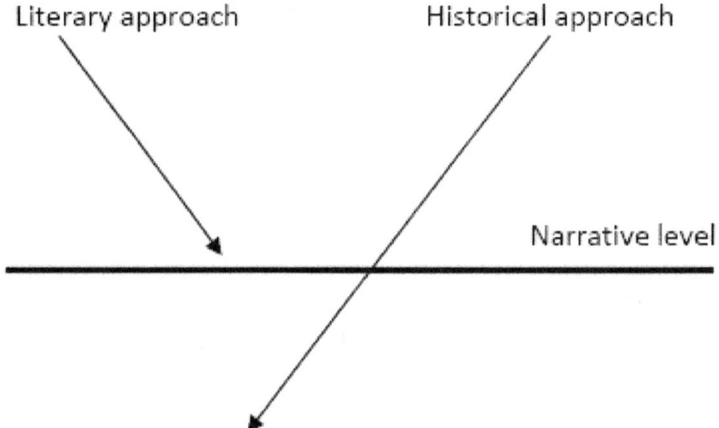

Those who are used to reading the Bible in churches often find it disconcerting the way historians selectively cite Biblical accounts, accepting some details as accurate while dismissing others as having insufficient evidence. It is important to recognize that this is not simply "picking and choosing" what one likes from the Bible, or at least it ought not to be that if historical methods are being faithfully applied. One detail from a

Gospel is included in a historical portrait of Jesus, while another is set aside, because the *evidence* for the historical accuracy of the two details is different.

Historical study is not the only way of approaching the Gospel, and depending what one hopes to accomplish, it may or may not be the best way. But if one wants to ascertain what we can know about Jesus as a historical figure with a high degree of probability, and what if anything is "beyond reasonable doubt," then historical study is the *only* way to accomplish that. Inevitably, some sayings and stories will have to be set aside as of questionable historical value, in particular if they are found in only one relatively late source. This does not in and of itself mean that historians have *disproved* those things. In some cases they may indeed have shown them to be highly unlikely, but in others there will simply not be sufficient evidence to decide the matter one way or the other. The distinction between those two categories is an important one, even if in the end both types of material are omitted from a historian's discussion of what we know about Jesus

The aim of all this is to uncover a core of information regarding Jesus that most historians, regardless of background or religious upbringing, should be able to agree is authentic. It is the need for such information that makes the use of these methods not merely helpful but essential. In the rest of this book, we shall apply the methods we have introduced here to the topic of the burial of Jesus of Nazareth, which is of ongoing interest, and not merely when new archaeological data comes to light.

Chapter 3
Death Before Dishonor: The Burial of the Historical Jesus

It is sometimes stated that the life of the historical Jesus ends with his death, and there is a sense in which this is true. Historical study can only provide access to the human life of Jesus, and his human life, like all human lives, ended when he died. When ancient Jews spoke of resurrection, they did not mean resuscitation, a restoration to ordinary human life, but rather they were referring to the final restoration of human beings to eternal life, expected at the end of history. Resurrection in that sense is *by definition* not an event like other events in human history. For this reason, stories about such an occurrence cannot be studied with the tools of historical study, either to confirm it or deny it. This does not mean, however, that one cannot attempt to evaluate the historicity of some of the events connected with the resurrection. For example, a historian *can* ask how strong the evidence is that the tomb was found empty that Sunday morning after the crucifixion. A historian can also describe the beliefs of early Christians about the resurrection inasmuch as they wrote about them, and can talk about the strong conviction that the Christians showed, indicating that they firmly believed Jesus had risen from the dead. But Christians today who have not themselves found an empty tomb or seen visions may nevertheless have the same sort of conviction. And so one cannot "prove the resurrection" by appealing to fervency of belief. In this chapter, we will consider what relevant data historical study *can* provide us with, which should be incorporated into discussions of and reflections on the resurrection.

It is Paul whose writings are the earliest of those included in the New Testament, and already in the time of Paul's connection with Christianity, less than a decade after the crucifixion, the cross and resurrection of Jesus were central to Paul's understanding of what Jesus had accomplished for humankind. These two events have remained connected and similarly important for Christians down the ages, even if not for precisely the same reasons and in precisely the same ways. But what can one say from a historian's perspective about these events? Ironically, the crucifixion is perhaps the most certain and easily verifiable historical datum of the whole story of Jesus, while the resurrection by definition lies beyond the reach of a historian's tools. But this should not deter us from going as far as we can with a historical investigation of these events, to which we now turn. We shall begin by discussing the crucifixion, albeit only briefly, so as to set our discussion of the burial of Jesus in its immediate context.

The Crucifixion

The brute fact that Jesus was executed by crucifixion is essentially beyond doubt. If there was anything that normally would have automatically excluded someone from serious consideration as having been the Davidic Messiah, the one anointed by God to restore the kingship to the line of David, it was being executed by the foreign power ruling over the Jews. As a result of these and other concerns, there were those within early Christianity who found the offense of the cross too much to bear and sought to deny that it had happened, while others dealt with it by denying the real humanity (and thus the sufferings) of Jesus. Such Christian beliefs, often referred to using the label *docetism*, mainstream Christianity branded heretical. But the very fact that Christians proclaimed their oxymoronic message about a "crucified Messiah" pretty much speaks for itself. It is simply not something that anyone in a Jewish context in that time would make up and then try to persuade their fellow Jews was true.

In addition, the Roman historian Tacitus records that Jesus was executed in the time of Pontius Pilate. The fact *that* Jesus was crucified is a secure and reliable piece of historical data. In turn, it indicates that, whatever Jesus may have said or thought about himself, his followers must have been strongly convinced that he was the Messiah. For them to have reached that conclusion *after* the crucifixion is unimaginable. And of course, for Jesus to have been crucified, he must have existed. For that reason, the suggestion that is sometimes made, namely that the figure of Jesus was completely and entirely invented by the early Christians, does not persuade professional historians.

Supplementing the New Testament accounts, we also have general information about the Roman practice of crucifixion. Christian tradition pretty much unanimously claims that there were female followers and supporters of Jesus present at the crucifixion. However, the cinematic depiction of them standing right next to the cross is not necessarily accurate. Mark says they watched from afar (Mark 15:40). It is thus a real possibility that any actual words Jesus spoke on the cross would have been inaudible, and whether he said anything at all would most likely have been unknown. To fill this gap, Mark 15:34 attributes to Jesus the appropriate words of Psalm 22 (the first verse was commonly quoted to indicate that the entire psalm was recited), while Luke 23:34 has Jesus practice what he preached and forgive those who did this to him. (Some manuscripts lack the famous phrase, but it is more easily explicable why it would have been removed than to account for it having been added, and the parallel with the story of Stephen in Acts seems to require it). John, with his view of Jesus as fully in control at all times, adds "I thirst" to fulfill prophecy, "Woman, behold your son…" and "It is finished" (John 19:26-30). Although there are ongoing debates about what medical factors were the most usual direct cause of death in cases of crucifixion, one common suggestion is asphyxiation, and if this is correct, then that makes it particularly likely that anything Jesus might have said while on the cross, particular towards the end, would have been inaudible and subject to being misheard. The Gospel of Mark in fact suggests this was the case (Mark 15:34-35). Matthew elaborates his depiction of the scene by drawing details from Wisdom of Solomon 2:12-21. All in all, the Gospels give us a core of historical information (Jesus was crucified) overlaid with theological interpretation, and further development of the narrative based on elements drawn from the Jewish Scriptures. The Jesus Seminar, it may be worth mentioning, rates all the sayings of Jesus on the cross as "black" (i.e. inauthentic).

The Death of Jesus

Do we know for certain that Jesus died when the Romans crucified him? For some, this may seem like a non-question. Although Muslims hold that Jesus was taken alive to heaven and was not crucified, most people in the Western world accept as a given that Jesus died on a cross. Whether we have heard it in the creeds, read it in the Bible, heard it from a televangelist while flipping channels, or seen it on the silver screen, that Jesus died is a strong presupposition which most of us share. Even though this presupposition is in all likelihood correct, historical study asks for evidence, and we must provide it here. We must also provide it because alternative accounts in which Jesus survives the crucifixion and heads for India or Japan (where one can find a tomb that is supposedly his) continue to receive media attention from time to time. Yet even apart from such claims, historians should always be open to reconfiguring and reconsidering evidence, to alternative possibilities, and the case of the death of Jesus is no exception.

Was it even *possible* to survive crucifixion? The answer is yes. The strongest evidence comes from Flavius Josephus, a Jewish historian who wrote around the same time as some of the New Testament Gospels are thought to have been written, and who has things to say about John the Baptist, James the brother of Jesus, and probably about Jesus himself (although his testimony has been expanded by Christian copyists, so that what Josephus himself wrote has been obscured from view). Josephus participated in the Jewish war against Rome that ended with the destruction of the Temple in Jerusalem in the year 70 C.E. When he was captured, he predicted that Domitian would become emperor, and his life was spared. At one point he came across some of his friends who had been captured by the Romans and were in the process of being crucified. He petitioned for them to be taken down from their crosses, and one of them managed to survive (*Life of Flavius Josephus* 75.420-421). It was therefore possible to survive crucifixion at least in cases where the crucified individual was taken down relatively quickly from the cross.

As has long been noted, the stories of Jesus' crucifixion suggest that he was taken down after having died remarkably quickly. Some have suggested that the vinegar he was given to drink was in fact a drug, which was used by his supporters to feign his death so that he could be taken down from the cross more quickly and then be revived. This possibility is not to be dismissed lightly simply because the story of Jesus' *death* is more familiar and taken for granted to such a large extent, or because of theological presuppositions about the Bible's truthfulness. It is certainly possible that key details in the later Gospels, such as the statement that Jesus' side was pierced by a Roman soldier, may have been added precisely to counter the claim that Jesus could have survived the crucifixion. Perhaps, at that very time when literate individuals around the Roman empire were reading about Josephus' experience, this accusation arose and inspired the author of the Fourth Gospel to provide literary "proof" that Jesus had died.

But a literary statement is not itself historical proof, and in some cases, when a later author adds a detail, it may be precisely because of, and a direct response to, a claim to the contrary. Indeed, a historian sometimes has no way of knowing whether a literary work tells the most widely known version of a story, or represents a desperate attempt to counter the generally accepted or most widely circulated version with a new one.

In the case of the question we are asking here about the death of Jesus, the answer will not be provided by simply reading the Gospel accounts. We must add to this evidence a number of other crucial historical considerations. First, the Romans were quite adept at execution, and it seems unlikely that friends of Jesus would have been able to give him a drug to cause him to appear dead, thereby outwitting the Romans. Were this a viable option, presumably it would have been tried before/subsequently and the Romans would have caught on, leaving some mention in a source from the Roman era. Second, and more important, is the consideration that Jesus' followers were willing to give their lives in later years for their conviction that Jesus had not simply survived death, but had been raised from death and seated at God's right hand. Such testimony does not prove that they were right, but it does suggest that they genuinely believed what they claimed. They also admitted, and at times boldly proclaimed, that Jesus had been crucified and died. This last piece of evidence is crucially important. Most people in that time would have assumed that crucifixion by the Romans was a clear indication that someone was *not* the Davidic Messiah. It is the closest thing one can imagine to an automatic disqualification. Had Jesus survived the Romans' attempt to execute him, *that* would surely have become a centerpiece of Christian proclamation.

Later in this book we shall discuss the question of what basis the early Christian proclamation of the resurrection had in the experience of Jesus' followers. At this point it is sufficient to note that their *conviction* that Jesus had died and risen seems to correctly presuppose that *he did in fact die*. Of course, one can always argue that there was a conspiracy involving just a few trusted individuals, who gave Jesus the drug while he was on the cross, and rescued him from the tomb later on, with most of his disciples being none the wiser. But from the perspective of historical study, the weight of probability seems to be clearly in favor of Jesus having died. Historical study is about assessing probabilities, and one error that many armchair historians make is to assume that all that is needed is to come up with a scenario that is *not impossible* while showing that other views are *not absolutely certain.* If historians proceeded in that way, we would be able to feel confident about almost nothing. Historical study is about making the best attempt we can to determine what is *most likely to have happened.*

Many discussions of the end of Jesus' life make the mistake of jumping directly from Jesus' death to questions about his resurrection. We will not, however, have all the necessary historical information at our disposal until we consider his burial. It is here, perhaps, more than anywhere else, that a historian's perspective and popular thought (including much Christian storytelling and art) dramatically part company. And it is the tendency to neglect this crucial element that is the reason for the existence of the book you are now reading.

The Burial of Jesus

Although the historical *life* of Jesus, or perhaps better the life of the historical Jesus, ends when he dies, as in most cases, a historian may have more to say, since the *burial* of Jesus, and/or anything else that may have been done to his body, also lies within the realm of that which may be historically investigated. Our earliest account of Jesus' burial, the Gospel of Mark, records a fundamental truth that later Christian authors tried desperately to obscure: Jesus' disciples were not in a position to provide Jesus with an honorable burial. Mark tells us that a pious Jewish leader named Joseph of Arimathea made sure that Jewish law was observed and, learning that Jesus had died, he got permission to take the body and bury it. Jewish law forbade that a body should be left exposed overnight, and although some historians have suggested that Jesus might not have even been buried, Josephus once again provides evidence of Jewish practices and concerns in his time. In his book *The Jewish War* (Book 4, chapter 5) Josephus explicitly condemns the impiety of Idumeans who cast away dead bodies without burial, whereas for Jews burial was so important that that they even "took down those that were condemned and crucified, and buried them before the going down of the sun" (2.317). Joseph of Arimathea was thus acting out of concern for the observance of the Jewish Law and Jewish burial customs.

Did he have deeper motives? In Mark's Gospel, Joseph has not yet been turned into a disciple of Jesus, as he would eventually be in some of the Gospels that were written later. Here he is simply a pious Jew, one who (like so many others) was eagerly expecting the Kingdom of God, and who as a righteous individual sought to ensure that Jewish scruples about the burial of the dead were implemented. May he have had some sympathy for Jesus, as later sources suggest? While this is not impossible, neither can it be considered probable. He was certainly in no sense a disciple of Jesus as far as any observable behavior on his part might indicate. He did not even allow the collaboration of the women who followed Jesus, and who would gladly have helped give Jesus an honorable burial to whatever extent this was possible and permissible. On the contrary, in our earliest account in the Gospel of Mark, we are told that Joseph did only the absolute bare minimum required: he wrapped the body in a cloth, with no mention of even washing the body, much less anointing it. This explains why Mark included the story in Mark 14:3-9 about the woman who poured perfume over him: Jesus was thereby anointed beforehand for burial, and this made up for the fact that the disciples were not given the opportunity to do so later. Mark's details need to be compared with John 19:39-40, which contradicts the earlier accounts at this point, and depicts Joseph as a disciple who provides Jesus with an honorable burial. Acts 13:29, however, appears to confirm what we have thus far argued was the case: it attributes the burial of Jesus to the Jewish leaders acting together, as their final action against Jesus.

Leaving to one side the apologetic statements of the later Gospels, which emphatically assert that Jesus was placed in a new tomb that had never been used before, and was wrapped in a *clean* linen sheet, we are only told in Mark's Gospel that Jesus was placed in "a tomb." We may surmise that this was a tomb near the execution site, used for the burial of criminals. It would presumably have needed burial niches to accommodate significant numbers of corpses at one time. Tombs of this sort are mentioned in rabbinic literature some centuries later. The custom was for bodies to be allowed to decompose for a year in rock tombs, after which time families would in most instances have been allowed to remove the bones of their loved ones and deposit them in their family tomb, assuming the crime was not such that even an honorable secondary burial was disallowed.

Joseph of Arimathea himself probably did not touch the body, and so he buried Jesus the same way "Solomon built the temple" – by arranging for others to do it. This is presumably why the Gospels refer to the place where "they" laid him, although this might also reflect the fact that Joseph acted under the authority of and as a representative of the Jewish ruling council. That the Jewish authorities would have been concerned about observing the Law in having Jesus buried may seem strange to some Christian readers, who have been influenced by the Gospels' depiction of the Jewish leaders as actively seeking Jesus' death, allegedly even being willing to break their own laws in order to bring this about. Yet here too a historian will have difficulty with a straightforward reading of the Gospel accounts. In the time of Jesus there was no C-SPAN, and there is no reason to expect that any of Jesus' followers actually knew what transpired after Jesus was apprehended by the Jewish authorities. They were almost certainly not privy to the discussions that took place between the high priest and other council members. What the Gospels do seem to agree on, however, is that Jesus was apprehended and almost immediately turned over to the Romans. If Jesus were wanted for breaking the Jewish

Law, or was sought by the Jewish authorities because of their own interest in him as a troublemaker, then we would have expected them to put him in prison until the Passover had ended, and deal with him then. That they instead brought him immediately to the Romans indicates what historians, who know the political realities of the time, would anyway have suspected: it was, in fact, primarily the *Romans* who wanted Jesus apprehended, and the Jewish authorities were taking preemptive action to hand Jesus over to them, lest the Romans send their troops in and there be more bloodshed and loss of life.

In John 11:47-49, the Jewish high priest is depicted as saying precisely that. Anyone who gathered crowds was considered dangerous. If there was talk and speculation that God might restore David's dynasty by making a particular individual king, the Romans would be all the more interested in eliminating that person. The Jewish authorities, as John indicates, acted out of concern to save more lives by sacrificing one. However one may feel about this course of action, it is certainly not incompatible with their being concerned about the observance of the Jewish Law regarding the burial of the dead before sundown.

One may suppose (as the Gospels also indicate) that the female followers of Jesus who were present at the crucifixion were interested to note where Jesus was buried. They would, at the very least, wish to come back to the tomb after the Sabbath to give him the decency of the minimal elements of a Jewish funeral: to mourn him (assuming this was not prohibited by Jewish law in that time), perhaps to anoint the body (although whether they would have attempted this after the body had had an opportunity to begin to decompose is uncertain), and presumably to note where in the tomb his body was, so that they could collect the bones later and give them a respectful burial, placing them in an ossuary (a "bone box") in his family tomb, or at the very least in something other than a grave for criminals.

They may have wished to do more than this. That the disciples should have been suspected of stealing the body (see Matthew 28:11-15) was not simply an attempt to counter Christian claims about the resurrection. Many people would have expected Jesus' disciples to take his body and give an honorable burial to their master. Jewish law in later times explicitly prohibited the burial of executed criminals in their family tomb, and even prohibited performing the customary mourning for those executed. Whether such laws existed in the time of Jesus is unclear, but the *Gospel of Peter* depicts the authorities as prohibiting mourning for executed criminals (see verses 50-54). Moreover, the account in Mark's Gospel itself seems to suggest that some of the concerns of later Jewish laws preserved in rabbinic sources existed in the time of Jesus. Indeed, they are applied very precisely by Joseph of Arimathea: he seeks to obey the Torah's injunction that bodies not be left exposed overnight; he does not give Jesus' body to Jesus' family; and he places the body in "a tomb" that was right by the execution site, which suggests that it was a tomb used for precisely the purpose of burying those executed nearby, as Jewish law required. All of this is believable to a historian not only because it comes from our earliest source and matches information from later Jewish law, but also because the early Christians who told the story of Jesus' burial found this information embarrassing and uncomfortable, and sought to change the impression given by the story when they retold it later. That a story which made a group uncomfortable is unlikely to have been invented by that group is a common principle used by historians to assess the plausibility of information provided in historical sources.

Methinks they do protest too much: Later Additions of an Apologetic Character

We will now consider elements included only in later Gospels, which strike a historian as attempts to make the burial of Jesus appear to have been more honorable than it actually was. Such details regularly *contradict* earlier sources, but at the very least they are *absent* from the earliest passion narrative, that in the Gospel of Mark. In each case, a historian will ask why that detail was added to the earlier account, and why emphasis is placed upon it in the later author's retelling of the story. Why emphasize that the linen sheet was *clean* and the tomb *unused*, for example (Matthew 27:58-59)? Presumably because there was a version of story already circulating in which the contrary was either assumed or explicitly stated. Often, emphatic assertions are important clues to what others were saying, even when those other voices left no written accounts of their side of the story. Let us now look at a few examples of these later additions of an apologetic character.

- *The tomb as unused*

Why would later authors emphasize this point? Perhaps because Jesus was indeed buried in a nearby grave used for those executed on the site. As important as it was for the Romans to not merely execute but dishonor their victims through crucifixion, so much more was it important to law-observant Jews to obey the divine commandment that bodies not be left exposed overnight (Deuteronomy 21:22-23). The Romans were aware of uniquely Jewish scruples, and in some cases made allowances for them. For instance, the Romans refrained from displaying in Judea the symbols of Roman power which the Jews regarded as idolatrous, and which were found absolutely everywhere throughout the rest of the Roman empire. Had the Romans regularly refused the Jews the right to bury even the crucified, we would expect there to be more complaining about it in Jewish literature from the time.

Josephus, however, who condemns the Idumeans for not burying the dead, had a favorable view of the Romans. While one does not need to be overly cynical to attribute this to the fact that the emperor was Josephus' patron, it still seems unlikely that Josephus would have criticized the Idumeans for something of which his Roman patrons were also guilty. There is thus no reason to think that the Romans regularly refused requests for permission to bury the dead before sundown on the day of death.

Burial in a common grave for criminals was itself dishonorable, even thought not nearly as much so as being denied burial altogether. For this reason, later Christians considered it important to honor Jesus by giving him as honorable a burial as possible in their literary depictions of the event. That they would do this, even though they were convinced that Jesus had been raised from the dead (which in and of itself would be understood as God himself "overturning" the verdict on Jesus and his execution), shows just how important burial was in this historical and cultural context.

- *The tomb as Joseph of Arimathea's own*

This detail is found only in Matthew's Gospel, and only makes sense when coupled with his depiction of Joseph as a disciple (Matthew 27:57-60). Yet as we have already emphasized, if he had truly been a disciple or even sympathetic to Jesus' movement, we would have expected to see in our sources something like the incident famously depicted in Michelangelo's Pieta, where Mary is allowed to hold her son's body after it is taken down from the cross, and presumably thereafter allowed to participate in the burial of her son. But in fact, in the canonical Gospels we are made to understand that Jesus' mother is *not* given the body, since his relatives and female followers are left at a distance, uninvolved in the burial. While Joseph being a "*secret* disciple" (as some sources suggest) might account for his failure to involve other disciples, his failure to allow Jesus' mother and other female family members the right to participate in the process is unintelligible if Joseph had an entirely favorable attitude towards Jesus. And if he had not in historical reality been a disciple (secret or otherwise), we would not expect him to bury Jesus in his own tomb. When we add to these considerations the fact that a member of the ruling council would be unlikely to have a tomb on a site used by the Romans for executions, it seems beyond reasonable doubt that Jesus was *not* buried in Joseph of Arimathea's own tomb. Here too, we are dealing with an attempt by later followers of Jesus to honor him in their *depiction* of the burial, in a way his disciples had been unable to in historical reality.

- *The anointing of the body by Joseph and Nicodemus*
As we progress further in the developing tradition, we find in the Gospel of John a depiction of an honorable burial for Jesus that not only goes beyond anything

indicated in the other Gospels, but directly contradicts them. Mark's earlier account has a woman pour perfume on Jesus, which is interpreted as her anointing him for burial beforehand (Mark 14:3-9; note how John 12:3-8 is forced to change the wording of what Jesus says here, with awkward results). The reason for making so much of this detail can only be that Jesus was not otherwise anointed for burial. This is confirmed explicitly in Mark's Gospel, which has the women go to the tomb on Sunday morning *to anoint the body* (Mark 16:1). If anything like what John depicted had actually happened, then the action of the women in Mark's Gospel makes no sense.

We may ask at this point whether the depiction of women going alone to the tomb early Sunday morning to anoint Jesus' body is itself believable, in view of the historical understanding of the burial of Jesus we have put forward thus far. Why do our sources tell us that there were no men present in the group that first went to the tomb? If you had been a disciple of Jesus, and he had been given a dishonorable burial, would you have been content to anoint his body and leave it in a tomb for common criminals? The reason why the story which circulated about the disciples stealing the body made sense is because many people would have expected them to do just that. For this reason, the argument one often hears, that the women going to the tomb by themselves makes their testimony more credible (since the testimony of women did not count for much in this ancient context) is problematic. Another possibility presents itself, namely that it was the intention of the disciples (both male and female) to move the body and give Jesus a decent burial. If so, the reason women alone are mentioned is that women would not be sought out by the authorities for going to the tomb, even if they might have tampered with it or intended to do so. Only males would be sought out and charged. That was the nature of this patriarchal society, with its value system based on honor and shame.

It is to be noted that we are only suggesting that the disciples may have indeed *wished* or even *intended* to steal the body. None of this should be taken to indicate that the Gospels are anything but honest when they say that the disciples were too late, that when they got to the tomb, Jesus' body was no longer there. Whether the tomb was in fact *empty* – that is, whether there were *no* bodies of other executed criminals present in the tomb – is something we cannot answer. The Gospels themselves do not say as much – they only claim that *Jesus'* body was not found there. And this is indeed the most likely historical scenario. Given the importance of a proper burial, it is hard to imagine that they would have refrained from telling the story of how they in fact accomplished that, in spite of everything that conspired to prevent it. Indeed, when we consider the lengths to which they were willing to go in rewriting the story, so as to give Jesus an honorable burial in their various retellings of it, the most likely explanation of this evidence is that they desperately desired to give Jesus a different sort of burial than he actually received, but were unable to.

Of course, other possibilities remain that may also be compatible with the evidence. Perhaps the male disciples fled Jerusalem as soon as they could, and after the Sabbath was over only female disciples remained to do what they could with the body, if anything. Neither can it be excluded entirely from the realm of possibility that the disciples *succeeded in removing and reburying the body*, and that this subsequent honorable burial influenced the later retellings of the story. Historical study cannot prove this was not what happened. All it can determine is that this scenario is *less likely* when compared to other reconstructions. For unless one can make a strong case for Jesus having had wealthy and influential supporters who lived in Jerusalem or its immediate vicinity, then we might have to conclude that Jesus' followers would at that time have had no other tomb to which they could move the body, however much they might have wanted to.

If the disciples did not steal the body, then is there another natural, historical explanation of why the tomb was empty? It is certainly highly implausible that the Jewish authorities would have obeyed the Law in burying Jesus, only to then remove it in violation of the Law. Most accounts have the women go to the tomb while it is still dark (Matthew 28:1; Luke 24:1; John 20:1), although Mark's account has them go to buy spices first (Mark 16:1-2). Modern readers tend to think of the day beginning at daybreak, and that the women went to the tomb at that time. However, in Jewish reckoning the Sabbath had ended at sundown the night before, and it is not entirely clear whether their trip to the tomb very early on the first day of the week means immediately after sundown or early the following morning. Depending on how one answers this question, there might have been time for someone else to remove the body. Yet at this point, if we are right in surmising that at least some of the disciples wished to move Jesus' body, it is more likely that they went to the tomb as soon as possible after the Sabbath was over. Mark's mention of them buying spices may be part of his attempt to portray them as wishing merely to anoint the body rather than relocate it. At any rate, it seems relatively certain that no observant Jews would have removed the body prior to the disciples getting there, since it was still the Sabbath, and the disciples would presumably have headed for the tomb as soon as the Sabbath was over. If Mark's information is taken at face value, however, then other possibilities become viable.

Is it imaginable that the Romans might have re-opened the tomb to bury (or simply toss in) one of the other individuals who were executed at the same time as Jesus, but died later than he did? Could we imagine Roman soldiers neglecting to replace the stone at the tomb's entrance, or even going so far as to intentionally not do so, thereby allowing scavengers to devour and defile the bodies, disgracing the criminals in death as the Romans considered appropriate? None of this would have been observed either by the Jewish authorities or Jesus' followers, as it would presumably have taken place on the Sabbath. However, the question of why the body was not in the tomb is a historical question that we cannot hope to answer with any degree of certainty using the tools of historical study. Prior to the highly supernatural description in the Gospel of Peter sometime in the second century of our era, we have no actual account of the departure of Jesus' body from the tomb, whether by natural or supernatural means. We only have stories of the tomb being found without Jesus' body in it at a later time. In terms of historical study, it will *always* be more likely that there is a natural explanation for the disappearance of Jesus' body, than that something supernatural, unprecedented and unparalleled in human history occurred.

Any person hearing of a missing body in our time would agree that an explanation in natural terms, however unlikely, is still *more probable* than an explanation in supernatural terms. The same rules as we apply to occurrences today must be applied consistently to events in the past, whether they occur in literature that some regard as sacred or not. This is yet another working principle of historical study. Indeed, in the Gospel narratives themselves, the initial reaction of the disciples, when they find the stone rolled away and

Jesus' body no longer there, is to assume that someone had moved the body. Even then, a missing corpse, in the absence of other considerations, was given a rather mundane explanation. As we shall see later, however, the question of what happened to Jesus' body is *not* the same question as whether God raised him from the dead. It is not even the same *sort* of question. We shall return to this topic in the next chapter.

- The guards at the tomb

One last change to the story of Jesus' burial requires mention. It not only differs from but actually contradicts earlier accounts, and yet Christian apologists still regularly make much of it. I am referring to the detail found only in the Gospel of Matthew, claiming that the authorities placed a guard on the tomb (Matthew 27:62-66).

There are obvious problems with this information from a historical perspective. To begin with, Matthew depicts the Jewish authorities as fully aware of and comprehending the meaning of Jesus' words about rising on the third day, while the Gospels are pretty much unanimous in agreeing that even Jesus' own disciples did not understand this until later and with the benefit of hindsight. The fact that this story explicitly attempts to counter a rumor circulating in Matthew's own time should likewise make us wary: he clearly had apologetic motives for telling this story, and these motives may have been sufficient in his mind to justify *creating* the story. In other words, rather than Matthew's story about the guarded tomb proving that the disciples could not have stolen the body, Matthew may have created this story precisely to counter such accusations.

Moreover, the problems created by having the women go to a guarded tomb are serious, and yet no one except Matthew mentions this fact. Moreover, according to Matthew, rather than finding the stone already rolled away (Mark 16:4), an angel did it as they arrived (Matthew 28:2), thus dealing with the guards as well. Since the guards on the tomb made it impossible for the women to be going there to anoint Jesus' body, as the Gospel of Mark had stated, Matthew changes their reason for going there, so that we are told they simply wanted to *look at* the tomb (Matthew 28:1). Given that all of these details are found only in Matthew, and their introduction into the story forces him to alter what was found in his earlier source (i.e. the Gospel of Mark), a historian cannot but regard these details with skepticism. Certainly they are not things that can be proven "beyond reasonable doubt." On the contrary, they are very much in doubt themselves, as far as their historical factuality is concerned.

In raising the issue of *doubt*, it is perhaps appropriate to mention here the conclusion of Matthew's Gospel, which depicts the encounter of eleven apostles with the risen Jesus in Galilee. Matthew's Gospel itself says that some of those who were there when the risen Jesus appeared *doubted* (Matthew 28:17). And so to claim to prove the resurrection "beyond doubt" in our time is to claim to be able to attain a degree of certainty that eluded even those disciples who are said to have been there and seen for themselves.

The Talpiot Tomb: How Many Times Was Jesus Buried?

As was mentioned earlier, the practice in the time of Jesus was for the body of a person to be placed in a tomb for a year, while the body decomposed, and then for the bones to be gathered up and placed in an ossuary or "bone box" in the family tomb. While in most instances both initial and secondary burial took place in a family tomb, later Rabbinic law makes the case of criminals an exception, and states that they are to be buried in a grave specifically for criminals, and only after a year had passed would the family be allowed to remove the bones and deposit them in their family tomb. Only rarely have discussions of the burial of Jesus (whether in relation to the Talpiot tomb or more generally) dealt with this custom and its relation to both the textual and the archaeological evidence.

The place where Jesus' body was placed after his crucifixion could in theory have been one of three things. First, it may have been a trench grave, much of the sort we use today, which was the most common manner of burial among the poor. Second, it may have been a tomb for criminals, perhaps in a nearby cave. Finally, it may have been a tomb owned by someone and used for their family for purposes of both initial burial and thereafter the secondary depositing of the bones of the deceased in ossuaries.

We have already seen problems with the last scenario, which envisages Joseph of Arimathea placing Jesus in his own family tomb, something depicted in Matthew alone. The consistent references to Jesus having been placed in a tomb would seem to rule out the first possibility, although our earliest source, the letters of Paul, only refer to him having been *buried*, without providing further details (1 Corinthians 15:4), and so it cannot be ruled out entirely. Nevertheless, the most likely scenario is that Jesus' body was placed in a nearby tomb reserved specifically for those who were executed at that site. Given the number of people executed by the Romans in this period, it would certainly have been more convenient in many respects to have a single cave tomb used for burying those who were executed, than to provide for their burial in trench graves on each occasion. How close to the surface the bedrock was in a given area would also have been a factor that influenced the method of burial used, and cave and rock hewn tombs seem to predominate in the Jerusalem area.

If Jesus' disciples *had* stolen the body, and if the Talpiot tomb were the final resting place of the bones of Jesus of Nazareth, then *how many times would his body or bones have to have been moved for this to be the case*? After initially being placed in a common tomb as indicated above, Jesus' family and/or disciples would have had to move it to another tomb used for primary burial. This could not have been the Talpiot tomb, since there is no evidence that Jesus' family prior to Easter lived in Jerusalem, much less owned a family tomb well outside it (which is where the Talpiot neighborhood would have been in the first century). They would thus have needed to find another tomb for initial burial. Then they would have wanted to rebury Jesus' bones a year later, which still seems too early for the family of Jesus to have established such a presence in Jerusalem. Eusebius of Caesarea (in Book II of his famous history of the church) makes reference to a monument for James the brother of Jesus in the vicinity of the site of the Temple in Jerusalem, which is indicative of his status after a lifetime spent leading the Jerusalem church and after being murdered and regarded as a martyr. Even in this instance, however, the reference is to a monument or *stele*, presumably marking the place of James' burial in a trench grave, rather than to a *tomb*. If at the end of his life he did not have a family tomb to be buried in, how plausible is it that his family had such a tomb in Jerusalem at the time of Jesus' death or within the year or so immediately following that?

It not impossible that someone donated a tomb for Jesus, either immediately after the crucifixion or at some later point. Yet who would do such a thing, if not one or more of his followers or sympathizers? And for Jesus to have been buried in Jerusalem unbeknownst to most of his followers, we would have to imagine this person on the one hand being involved in the Jesus movement, while on the other hand simultaneously being involved in a conspiracy to hide information from other Christians and from the general populace. Once again, this scenario is not impossible, but from a historical perspective, one must ask whether it is *more probable* than other scenarios, as well as whether the textual accounts that tell a very different story make sense as either as attempts to cover up this series of moves of Jesus' body, or as the writings of followers who were ignorant of what had really happened to Jesus' body and bones. It is altogether appropriate to ask whether a corpse could have been moved as many times as this theory requires without more people knowing about it, and without it leaving traces in our textual records, even if only in the form of an apologetic *denial* that they had moved the body on more than one occasion. Given that the burial Jesus received (as described in our earliest Gospel, the Gospel of Mark) made Christians so uncomfortable that they consistently tampered with the story, it is more likely that this Gospel's information is more-or-less indicative of what actually happened, and that the

Talpiot tomb is in fact the tomb of someone else named Jesus or Joshua, whose father's name also happened to be Joseph.

Lessons in Family History

Anyone who has spent hours poring over parish registers as they researched their family history can attest just how frequently one encounters the same names one is seeking, only to discover later that the individuals in question were not the ancestors you were looking for. If one extrapolates this back roughly two millennia into the time of Jesus, when there were no surnames but only nicknames, patronymics and places of birth to distinguish people of the same name, it becomes clear just how insignificant it is that a tomb was found that includes names such as "Jesus son of Joseph" and "Mary". Although there have been many conflicting claims about the odds and the statistical probabilities or improbabilities of this particular combination of names, all the evidence suggests that we should expect to find this combination of names again, probably more than once, before we are done recovering all the ossuaries that might exist in the regions of Judea and Galilee from the time of Jesus. Mary was the most common female name in this period, and both Joseph and Joshua/Jesus were in the top ten.

The family of Jesus of Nazareth was not limited to his mother Mary and his brother James, nor was their influence in positions of leadership limited to the first generation of Christians. Relatives of Jesus continued to be mentioned in early Church sources for some time thereafter, and it is hard to account for this in conjunction with the identification of the Talpiot tomb as the tomb of Jesus of Nazareth. Could the existence of such a tomb as a *family tomb* for Jesus have been kept secret from the members of his own family? If it was known to the members of his family, how do we account for their prominent involvement in a movement claiming that after the crucifixion his body had not been found? The conspiracy that one would have to posit becomes ever increasingly complex, and although I do not wish to rule out altogether the possibility of conspiracies in early Christianity, when the secret-keeping of the conspirators begins to appear more miraculous than a resurrection, it is time to abandon such an approach and seek more plausible historical explanations of what happened.

The Church of the Holy Sepulcher

The Talpiot tomb is unlikely to be the final (or, since the ossuary bearing the inscription “Jesus son of Joseph” was empty, the penultimate) resting place of the bones of Jesus of Nazareth. How likely is it that the traditional site, the Church of the Holy Sepulcher, represents the place where Jesus' body was first buried? The church was built under the auspices of the Emperor Constantine, on the basis of local lore identifying it as the site of Golgotha, the place where Jesus was crucified and buried. At that time a temple to Aphrodite stood there, which had to be demolished in order to see whether the tomb was beneath it. It seems fairly unlikely that local Christians would have invented a claim that their holy site was beneath a pagan temple, and thus the identification of the site as Golgotha probably went back to at least some time before that temple had been built. Beneath it the emperor's men apparently found a cave and were persuaded it was indeed the correct site. While it is unclear what about it persuaded them, it may be that in addition to finding tombs they found one in particular that bore the graffiti of earlier generations of pilgrims who had visited the site. In most cases graffiti and people carving their names on a sacred site are things the pious would frown upon, but when such etchings remain over the centuries, at times they can prove quite valuable in making identifications, as well as in studying the piety of earlier generations of religious believers.

Prior to the time of Jesus, the site had been a limestone quarry, and there is evidence that it was no longer in use as such in his day and age. It may have been the protrusion of white rock that led to it being nicknamed “the place of the skull”, and it has even been suggested that its status as an *abandoned* quarry may have inspired Christian use of the verse “the stone the builders rejected has become the cornerstone” in reference to Jesus (Psalm 118:22, quoted in Mark 12:10 and parallels). At any rate, sometime after it ceased to serve as a quarry, it presumably began to serve as a site for executions and burials. At present, there is no way to know for certain whether this is the actual site of the tomb, although further investigations of the “edicule,” which is supposed to incorporate the original rock-cut tomb uncovered in the time of Constantine, may someday change this situation. Historians are pretty much agreed, however, that of the sites that have been proposed over the years for Golgotha and the tomb in which Jesus was buried, this is the only serious contender.

In building the Church of the Holy Sepulcher, they removed a significant portion of the rock surrounding the tomb they identified as that of Jesus. This process left a single tomb in the midst of the church, but may have removed other useful archaeological evidence in the process. It is clear, however, that this site was not the location of only a single small tomb. It might better be called a *graveyard*, with numerous tombs carved into the soft rock, some of which are still there beneath the church. One could imagine that, in an area with many tombs, in which there may even have been a network of passageways carved into the rock to allow for multiple burials, individuals who had not been involved in burying a particular body might have had difficulty locating it. Nevertheless, the determination and devotion of Jesus' followers, evidenced by their seeking the body in the first place, makes it unlikely that their failure to find the body was simply an oversight on their part. And so there is no obvious solution in terms of natural explanation to the mystery of what happened to the body of Jesus. The appropriate course of action in such a case, in terms of historical study, is not declare this proof of a miracle, but rather to state the following: historically speaking, we do not know what happened to Jesus' body.

History and Faith

Returning to the overarching theme of history and faith that ties this book together, what is the relationship between the two with respect to the empty tomb and the resurrection, based on what we have considered thus far? Historical study can indeed conclude that it is most likely that a group of disciples went to the tomb in which Jesus had been buried, early on the Sunday morning after the crucifixion, and that they did not find Jesus' body there. However, as was clear from the outset, historical study will never be able to state that it is more probable that Jesus' body was missing from the tomb for miraculous as opposed to ordinary reasons. Historical study deals with the ordinary, not in the sense that it does not indeed study extraordinary people doing extraordinary things in extraordinary circumstances, but in the sense that it deals with probability, and as Carl Sagan famously stated, extraordinary claims require extraordinary evidence. And since most religious believers would agree that resurrections are both unusual and improbable events, for that very reason no historian will ever be able to say "the body was *probably* missing because God raised Jesus from the dead."

To return to our metaphor of criminal investigations as in some ways parallel to historical study, how would it seem if a district attorney's office, after failing to figure out who killed a particular murder victim, issued a statement to the effect that, since no perpetrator has been identified, it is clear that God simply wanted the individual in question dead? No one (and particularly not taxpayers) would feel that this is an adequate or appropriate way to end a police investigation. This is not because we necessarily rule out in advance the possibility that God wanted the individual dead – indeed, many people would probably say about that individual, as about any other, that "God has his reasons" or "It was his time to go." We expect the police, detectives, and forensic experts, however, to work on the mundane, human level of cause and effect, and understand that theological interpretations of events are *a different sort of perspective*, which looks at the same events in another way or on another level that does not invalidate the level of the natural, on which level criminal investigations take place. The appropriate response of those investigating the crime is to leave the case file open. In the same way, if historians fail to account for the disappearance of Jesus' body from the tomb, the appropriate conclusions for them to draw *as historians* is that *we do not know for certain what happened to Jesus' body*. This is as far as historical study can take us with respect to this particular matter.

Although we shall treat the topic of the resurrection in the next chapter, it is appropriate in this context to draw attention to a few implications of our study thus far. Since historical study deals only in probability, if Christians' affirmation of Jesus' resurrection is about the historical question of what happened to his body after being placed in the tomb, then the most Christians can affirm is that the body of Jesus had *almost certainly* vanished, and they can further assert without transgressing the limits of historical inquiry that it is *possible* that Jesus rose from the grave. Clearly such language seems a poor and inadequate expression of Christian faith. The problem is not with either history or faith at this point. The problem is that Christians often wish to make *historical claims* without having sufficient *historical evidence*, as well as at times confusing *theological affirmations* with *historical* ones. The question will need to be asked therefore whether resurrection faith is really supposed to be about history at all, whether it is an affirmation about the whereabouts of a corpse. To many Christians, resurrection faith seems to be an affirmation of a different sort altogether. As we shall see in the next chapter, not only is what happened to the body *not* the decisive factor in resurrection faith; in many respects it is *irrelevant* to it.

Chapter 4
Jesus Beyond the Tomb

As we move into this chapter on the rise of early Christian belief in the resurrection, it is worth asking whether this continues to be a historical study at this stage, or whether we have now reached the point at which we must begin to move beyond historical study and make use of other tools and other perspectives.

On the one hand, as we shall see in this chapter, when early Christians spoke of Jesus as having been raised from the dead, they were not talking about his *resuscitation*, his restoration and return into life within history. On the contrary, the assertion that Jesus had been raised from the dead was an affirmation that Jesus had entered the age to come, a new kind of existence altogether, one that transcends history and what we might call space and time as we know them. Obviously, historical study by definition cannot hope to study that which lies outside of the bounds of historical existence. Yet on the other hand, it most certainly *is* possible for a historian, using the tools of historical investigation, to study and describe the early Christians' *beliefs about* the resurrection. Indeed, since their writings on this subject are expressed in ancient texts through the medium of ancient languages in concepts drawn from their ancient cultures and worldviews, it would be impossible to study their beliefs without the tools of historical inquiry. And it is altogether appropriate that, in preparing to reflect theologically about resurrection and its status as a component of Christian faith today, one first investigate not only the historical evidence regarding Jesus' tomb and burial, but also the historical evidence regarding the characteristics of early Christian faith in and beliefs about the resurrection. Indeed, a failure to investigate these matters before proceeding further would be to ignore the views of those whose testimony is for most Christians the most fundamental witness and most authoritative source when it comes to matters of faith and practice. Once we have surveyed what historical data there is of relevance to these subjects, we may then use that information as the basis for our further reflections.

It must be remembered as well that historical study is *descriptive* and not *prescriptive*. Historical study will only provide information about the past; the choice to *use* that information in some particular way will involve perspectives outside of and apart from historical study. Such a decision involves, among other things, our value judgments and theological presuppositions. And it is certainly not to be assumed that, just because we have described particular beliefs and practices among the earliest Christians, the appropriate course of action is to believe and act precisely as they did, as though that were even possible. To do so would represent a failure on our part to acknowledge the historical distance between ourselves and the first Christians, the changes in culture and worldview, in scientific knowledge and technology, and in many other aspects of our lives that inevitably separate us from them. Be that as it may, the appropriate starting point is to ask what we know about the beliefs of early Christians historically. Only having obtained such information can we ask what if anything one should do about it and how if at all one should respond to the information historians can provide regarding early Christianity.

The Resurrection Appearances

In the Gospels, finding an empty tomb does not lead to the belief that Jesus had been raised, but only to the conclusion that someone must have moved the body. Other experiences – of angelic apparitions, perhaps, or visions of Jesus – were necessary before the disciples drew the conclusion that something extraordinary and unexpected had taken place. In asking about the *nature* of these experiences, however, we cannot begin with the Gospels. Even if we did, the earliest New Testament

Gospel, the Gospel of Mark, in the earliest form in which we have it, does not include accounts of the risen Jesus being seen by anyone. Our earliest manuscripts of Mark end at 16:8, with the promise that Jesus will be seen in Galilee, but nothing more.

In the first instance, at any rate, we turn to early Christian writings that predate the Gospels, namely the letters of Paul. In 1 Corinthians 15, Paul places his own experience of seeing Jesus in the same category as the appearance of Jesus to the other apostles. While the Acts of the Apostles (written quite possibly a half a century or more later) tells the famous story of Paul's encounter with the risen Jesus on the Damascus Road three whole times (with occasional differences of detail, and some tension on the question of whether those with Paul heard but didn't see or saw but didn't hear), Paul's own writings do not provide any description of the experience that led him to become an adherent of the messianic Judaism he once persecuted. Paul does mention elsewhere, however, visionary experiences involving ascent into the heavens, which are very much characteristic of the mystical traditions and literature of that time (see 2 Corinthians 12:1-7).

What sorts of experiences did the very earliest Christians have that led them to assert that they had seen Jesus? Seeing visions of Jesus exalted to the heavens alone might not have been enough to convince them that he had undergone a *bodily* resurrection, but finding an empty tomb and then having such experiences may indeed have been sufficient to lead them to this conclusion. That their experiences were dreams and visions might lead some to assert that they were "merely psychological," but this is not necessarily a helpful way of putting the matter. That they were psychological really ought to be beyond dispute and uncontroversial, since no subjective experience that we have is unconnected to the functioning of our brains and our minds. But whether certain psychological phenomena are *merely* psychological is another question. Our experience of beauty, of wonder, of transcendence is firmly rooted in aspects of human psychology, but it is not necessary to conclude that it therefore tells us nothing significant, and perhaps even true, about the way the world is, about the nature of reality. Once again, we need to avoid confusing different levels of description and analysis. It should not be assumed that in offering a psychological or other scientific explanation of an experience, we have said everything important that one needs to know about it.

It is only fair to ask, however, whether the experience of Jesus' first followers in connection with his burial would itself have been enough to account for their dreams and visions, that is to say, to actually *cause* them. Imagine spending a few years of one's life following an individual who has announced that God's kingdom is about to dawn, that the fulfillment of all God's promises is at hand. In your heart, you entertain the hope that this individual is not just a teacher or even a prophet, but God's chosen one who will restore the kingdom of David and bring in the long-awaited messianic age. Yet, on what you hope may be the decisive occasion when all will be fulfilled, when he goes up to Jerusalem and makes more public than ever his messianic claims, he is apprehended and killed in a horrific manner, and finally buried without any of the honor he deserves, without any honor at all. In disappointment and despair, you go to the tomb as soon as you possibly can, hoping to at least do everything in your power to reverse this last injustice, but you find you are too late – his body has been taken away, and any hope of granting him dignity in death has been stolen from you. Can you be certain that such an experience would not have a psychological impact that might lead your subconscious to reassure you that in fact God had honored Jesus *beyond* death, had saved him from death and the dishonor of a criminal's tomb? If I am honest, I cannot say that such an explanation is entirely implausible. Yet I can say that the experiences of the disciples, to the extent that we have hints of them from their behavior as it was remembered and recorded by others, seem to have impacted them in thoroughly positive ways. They seem to have been experiences that were healing and positive, and the do not show signs of the effects we typically associate with a mental breakdown. Here, however, I am stepping outside my field: I am a Biblical scholar and a historian, and not a psychologist. But I am also a Christian, and can relate my own experience by way of analogy to that of the early Christians.

As a teenager, at a point in my life at which it seemed to me that my attempts to find happiness and meaning had failed, I was invited to a concert at a friend's church. Although I had considered myself a Christian, their worship seemed to have a reality about it that mine lacked. The next morning I attended the Sunday service, and (as in so many stories of this sort) I do not recall what the sermon was about. I do remember what happened at the end of the service, however. I prayed, calling out to God in total surrender, saying that my way of living clearly wasn't working, and whatever God's way was, I wanted to try it. At that moment, a sense of peace came over me, as though my burdens, uncertainties and sorrow had been lifted from off my shoulders. This is the experience that Christians today most frequently refer to in terms of being "born again," and I suspect that in addition to many of the generalities, some of the particulars will resemble experiences that others have had.

I am not certain whether the early disciples' experiences of "seeing Jesus" were experiences of this sort. My own experience did not include a visionary component, and it seems to me that the experience of resurrection appearances were more likely dreams, some of which may have been deeply unsettling in highlighting how they had failed their master, but others of which were presumably reassuring in that they conveyed to the disciples that God had vindicated Jesus and enthroned him in heaven. But what is interesting is that the Acts of the Apostles suggests that the experiences of seeing Jesus were not what turned this group of Christians into a bold movement proclaiming the resurrection and salvation. According to Acts chapter 2, it is the experience of an outpouring of the Holy Spirit that has this effect. This experience is described elsewhere in the New Testament as one that Christians more generally had, even those who did not claim to have found an empty tomb or have seen the risen Jesus. There is reason to think that these sorts of experiences more than anything else transformed the lives of Jesus' first followers, and then of others to whom their message spread, and persuaded all of them that Jesus was indeed alive.

Some readers who know the New Testament well will probably be reluctant to accept the claims made in this section. Speaking of the disciples' experiences of "seeing Jesus" as *dreams* and *visions* does not fit with some of the stories in the Gospels, in which Jesus even eats with people and was perhaps touched by them. However, it is important to observe that all such details which emphasize the physicality of Jesus' resurrection body are in the latest of the New Testament Gospels: Luke and John. The earlier Gospels do not specify that Jesus' resurrection body had this physical, material character, and our earliest Gospel, in its earliest form that we have access to, does not describe Jesus appearing at all.

Evidence for a Conspiracy?

There is one point at which, if one were inclined to make a case for some sort of conspiracy or cover up in connection with early Christianity, one could do so particularly plausibly. I am referring to the missing ending of Mark's Gospel. As all recent translations of the Bible point out, our earliest manuscripts end abruptly at Mark 16:8, after the phrase "they did not say anything to anyone, for they were afraid". There have been attempts to treat this ending as original. However, when we consider that copyists of the Gospel of Mark independently added at least two different endings, and that Matthew and Luke both felt the need to complete the story when they used Mark's Gospel, it seems clear that early readers of Mark's Gospel found its sudden ending at 16:8 unsatisfactory. Once we realize that it makes little or no sense to tell a story that ends with an assertion that no one was told about the events in the story, it begins to seem far more likely that the original version of Mark's Gospel must have once continued beyond this point.

Manuscripts were fragile, and it is certainly possible that the ending was lost by accident rather than by willful mutilation. Even if one posits a conspiracy, we have no idea what may have been in the lost ending, and so the cover up (if there was one) was successful. This, however, leads us on to one of the more troubling and disconcerting points that is indicated by a comparison of Mark's Gospel to those of Matthew and Luke. That it was the original version of Mark's Gospel that was truncated is clear from the fact that neither in any later copies of Mark, nor in Matthew's Gospel, nor in Luke's, do we see any indication of knowledge of this lost ending. Indeed, both Matthew and Luke depart significantly both from one another and from Mark at this point. Matthew follows Mark in keeping the reference to Jesus being seen *in Galilee*, announced by an angel, yet inserts an appearance of Jesus himself to the women immediately after that. This not only makes the angel's announcement redundant, but also makes it seem odd that Jesus does not appear to his disciples in Jerusalem. Luke's Gospel goes in an altogether different direction and has the disciples ordered to remain in Jerusalem, with that being the place where they see Jesus. It seems that Matthew and Luke did not already know the narrative that was found in the lost ending of Mark's Gospel. Whether they had no traditions about what happened next, or simply had very different ones, is unclear.

In chapter 15 of Paul's first letter to the Corinthians, Paul refers to the traditions he received and which he handed on to the churches he planted, concerning the resurrection appearances of Jesus. Sayings of Jesus and stories about him clearly were being circulated in the early church, and it is hard to imagine that the authors of later Gospels, in reading Mark's Gospel and using it as a source, had not already previously heard at least some of the stories and sayings of Jesus contained therein. How is it that, writing only a few decades later, these Gospel authors apparently had not heard Mark's story of the resurrection appearances of Jesus? How is it that they could diverge so thoroughly from one another at this point? Presumably they already knew traditions of Jesus having appeared to his disciples, and did not hear of this for the first time when they read Mark 16:7. Yet they seem not to have already known stories about these appearances that located them in a particular place – or at the very least, they knew stories that situated the appearances in different locations. The radical divergence of the stories Matthew and Luke tell at this point is disconcerting, to say the least.

If there was an "official" story stemming from the apostles in Jerusalem, it was presumably the one Paul was told, which is recorded in 1 Corinthians 15, and which lists the people who said they saw Jesus and does not specify *where*. The information Paul provides is certainly at least partially compatible with the traditions that other Gospels relate, namely that Jesus appeared to his inner circle of followers (whether in Galilee or Jerusalem) sometime soon after the crucifixion and the finding of the empty tomb. But it does not explicitly specify a time frame, other than that these appearances happened before Paul had his own experience of encountering the risen Jesus, and there are divergent views on when that occurred. Whether Paul's reference to the resurrection occurring on the third day (1 Corinthians 15:4) necessarily indicates that the disciples became *aware* that the resurrection had occurred on the third day also deserves further consideration.

Mark's Gospel, which in its present form ends with the reminder for Jesus' followers not reaching them ("they told no one anything, because they were afraid"), leaves open the possibility that some time passed before Jesus' disciples began to have visions or sightings of Jesus. Perhaps in this version, they did not expect to see him. Although in Mark 14:28, which is usually regarded as an addition by Mark to the earlier traditions he knew, Jesus tells the disciples to expect to see him, the disciples in Mark's Gospel regularly fail to understand what Jesus told them. They may thus have returned to their previous lives and work, only later encountering the risen Jesus and reuniting as a result. It is certainly not impossible that someone removed the ending of Mark's Gospel because it contradicted the "official" version of the story. Nevertheless, the Gospel of Mark's promise of resurrection sightings anticipates its fulfillment. And so, even though it might make sense to suggest that Mark's original ending was significantly different from the narratives included or alluded to elsewhere in the New Testament, it does *not* make sense to suggest that sightings of Jesus were altogether lacking. At the very least, it seems clear that the author knew stories about Jesus appearing, irrespective whether he wrote them in his Gospel in its original form.

We have already mentioned that Matthew and Luke both seem to depart significantly from Mark's story at precisely the point where our earliest manuscripts end. But this does not mean that the original ending of Mark has not left its mark (if you'll excuse the pun) on early Christian literature elsewhere. If, as we suggested, a plausible continuation of the story would involve the disciples returning to their homes in Galilee, we have two sources that tell just such a story. One is the early extracanonical work known as the *Gospel of Peter*. This work exists only in fragmentary form today, and as one of the earliest of Gospels not included in the New Testament, some scholars have suggested that it may incorporate oral tradition not included in or derived from the canonical Gospels. Where this fragment ends (for it is yet another Gospel that is missing its ending, and in this case most of its beginning as well), the reader has been told of the women's discovery of the tomb, their flight in fear, and then the story continues with the disciples returning to their homes, and Peter, Andrew and Levi take their nets and go to the sea. As for what may have happened next in the Gospel of Peter, or in the Gospel of Mark, we do not know for certain, but a plausible answer may be found in the final chapter of the Gospel of John.

Although we are not suggesting that the story found in John 21 *is* the lost ending of Mark, a plausible case can be made that it is based on the same tradition, and perhaps was even based on a knowledge of a complete manuscript of Mark's Gospel. It has often been noted that the story in John 21 makes better sense as the disciples' *first* post-resurrection encounter with Jesus, since it is hard to account for their return to their earlier lives and jobs after Jesus had appeared to them and commissioned them. It would, however, follow naturally after a story in which Jesus had risen but the women, out of fear, had not yet told anyone about their discovery of the empty tomb. Disillusioned, the male disciples return to their earlier lives, unaware of or forgetting the promise that they will see him in Galilee. Yet Jesus nevertheless meets them where they are. Further evidence for what we are proposing may be found in the fact that such a meeting by the sea would create what is known as an *inclusio*, a parallel between the beginning and ending, so that the first and last encounters of the disciples with Jesus in Mark would take place in the same seaside fishing setting. The appearance to Peter and the Twelve (if one removes the figure of the "beloved disciple," who is, as so often in the Gospel of John, inserted into the narrative where earlier sources do not leave room for him) would also match reasonably well with the information in our earliest source, 1 Corinthians 15.

If it was not clear already, hopefully as we have studied the Gospel endings it has become apparent that historical study of the post-Easter experiences of the first Christians is not simply a question either of reading all the sources that we have, or even simply accepting the information from the earliest ones. Historical study involves detective work. Sometimes older traditions pop up in later writings. In other cases, our earliest source or sources may be trying hard to present an alternative to a well-known account that is already circulating. When it comes to the subject of early Christian resurrection experiences, it may be that the earliest form of the "Easter story" involved the disciples returning to Galilee and encountering him there. While this may affect the role of the empty tomb in the rise of Christian belief in Jesus' resurrection, it also suggests that the experiences that led Jesus' dejected followers to believe this were powerful ones.

Stranger on the Shore

One can only speculate about what the first post-Easter experience of "seeing Jesus" may have been like. It is alluded to, but ultimately left undescribed, in 1 Corinthians 15:5, where Paul writes simply that he "appeared to Peter." The challenge to the historian is to reconstruct a plausible scenario that could have given rise to the evidence available in later sources. Perhaps, as we have suggested above, Peter returned to Galilee and to fishing. He wrestled with the failure of his expectations, with his own failure in denying Jesus, and perhaps with questions about whether things might have turned out differently had no one drawn a sword and cut off the ear of the high priest's servant (Mark 14:47). On one particular day he goes fishing, taking some of Jesus' other closest followers with him. They catch nothing, and much of the time is spent in silence. Then, they see a figure on the shore. The figure asks if they have caught anything, and they say no. He tells them to try again, and suggests a spot. They lower their net - and catch a huge number of fish. Peter makes a connection. Isn't this the spot where he first met Jesus, who did something similar on that occasion? He looks up. Perhaps the figure on the shore has already vanished. Perhaps he is still standing there, and they have breakfast without exchanging many words, as suggested in John 21. In either case, at some point after the figure has departed, Peter suddenly has a flash of insight: *it was Jesus*. He tells the others, but at least initially, they are skeptical, and for a time they remain unpersuaded.

Peter spends much of the days that follow in prayer, seeking information and advice from rabbis and experts in the Law. What do the Scriptures in fact say about what the Messiah would be like? Could the Messiah suffer? Could the Messiah return from the dead? Could the Messiah enter the messianic age of the resurrection ahead of everyone else? Were there passages that left open such possibilities, texts that had been neglected but which might allow for such an unthinkable, paradoxical, surprising Messiah? After much reflection, exploration and soul-searching, Peter contacts the rest of the Twelve, and they gather to hear what Peter has to say. They listen, and when he is done explaining to them what he has come to believe, he leads them in the prayer Jesus had taught them. "Father..." they begin. When they reach the words "Your will be done," they mean it as they had never truly meant it before. "Not our will, but yours." A sense of peace washes over them. A sense of certainty that Peter is right, that Jesus has in fact been raised. And in their dreams, and in glimpses in crowds, in mysterious encounters with unknown individuals, and even in mystical visions, they too experience this phenomenon of "Jesus appearing."

Could this be the way events unfolded, and Christian faith in the resurrection of Jesus arose? What we have written in this section is admittedly speculative. There seems to be little hope of gaining access by means of the later written sources to the actual experiences that early Christians had, the ones that convinced them Jesus was alive. Even Paul only alludes to his own direction-changing experience, and never describes it. Perhaps this is appropriate: religious experiences are regularly characterized by those who have them as ineffable, as "beyond words." The Gospel of Mark suggested that Jesus would be seen, but doesn't describe the experience, at least not in our earliest manuscripts. Our two earliest sources thus leave little for us to work with at this point.

But this much can be said: the act of completely surrendering has transformed many lives. Such unconditional surrender to God seems to have been central to Jesus' own spirituality. There would be something fundamentally appropriate if it turned out to be central to the rise in the earliest disciples of the conviction that Jesus had been raised, as it has been for Christians all through the ages since then. But even if we choose to speculate about the nature of these early Easter experiences, the truth is that, in the end, we do not have access to them. Those who have religious experiences often find words fail them. If we choose to fill the silence of our earliest sources with speculation, it should be speculation that respects the fact that those who have had religious experiences regularly acknowledge that, in the end, they defy description.

The End-of-the-World Character of Resurrection Belief

If there is particularly strong evidence for the remarkable character of the early Christian experiences (whatever the precise details may have been) which persuaded them that Jesus had been raised from the dead. The early Christians did not simply work through the implications of beliefs they already had. In some respects, the experiences that persuaded them of Jesus' resurrection and exaltation at the same time persuaded them to rethink other aspects of their worldview as well.

It has been suggested that, had these early disciples simply seen visions of Jesus, whether in their presence on earth or enthroned in heaven at God's right hand, this would most naturally have led to a belief that Jesus had been vindicated by God *spiritually*, without "undoing his death." This is not necessarily the case, however. Certainly the most common viewpoint in the Judaism of this time seems to have been that the dead remained in some sort of interim state, awaiting the end of the world and the final judgment (see, for example, 4 Ezra 7:75-101). On the other hand, the examples we have in the apocalyptic literature from this period of heavenly journeys by individuals are usually journeys by *living* individuals. This being the case, visions of Jesus enthroned at God's right hand *could* have been sufficient grounds for the early Christians to conclude that Jesus had been vindicated beyond death *by being raised from the dead.* It all depends, I suppose, on what the precise content of the visions and other experiences may have been. As we have already pointed out, in Paul's writings, there is no clear reference either to the empty tomb, or to an interim period wherein Jesus appeared physically as opposed to "merely" in visions. Paul places all the resurrection appearances in the same category as his own. And the metaphor that he uses in 1 Corinthians 15:35-44 (the mortal body as the seed that is planted, the resurrection body as the plant that sprouts from it) would work equally well, if not indeed better, if it were assumed that the body remained in the tomb. Be that as it may, what is certainly clear from the evidence is that the early Christians did not believe that Jesus simply joined the other dead in Sheol, which was the older Israelite concept of the "land of the dead." Their conviction was that he had been raised from death to life with God, the sort of life that most Jews expected would be experienced by righteous people who had died, not during an interim waiting period, but after the final resurrection and judgment.

This is where things get *really* interesting. There was no known prior concept within Judaism of an individual rising to eternal life prior to the final resurrection of all people at the end of time. Of course, there may have been some parallel in the case of Enoch, and perhaps also Moses. But in the case of Jesus, the early Christians' conviction that Jesus' resurrection had taken place caused them to rethink the whole timeline that they inherited from Judaism, regarding the unfolding of God's plan for the end of the world and the dawning of God's kingdom. Within Judaism, there was a clear concept of two ages. On the one hand, the present evil age is dominated by powers of darkness, sin and injustice. The age to come, on the other hand, also called the "messianic age" or the "kingdom of God," would involve the resurrection of the dead, the final judgment, and the restoration of paradise, from which all evil and suffering would be eliminated. These are often diagrammed as follows, with history progressing from left to right, so that as the present age is brought to an end, the age to come begins:

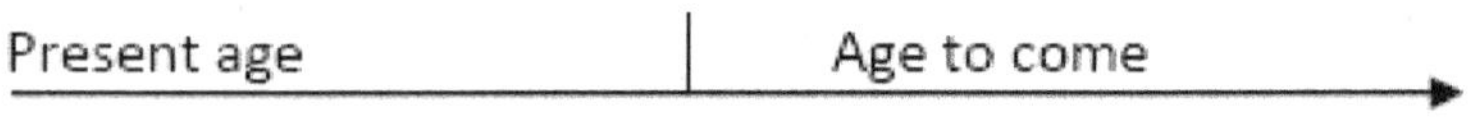

Present age | Age to come

The early Christians, starting from the conviction that Jesus had risen and thus that the final resurrection had begun, were forced to rework this schema. If Jesus had been raised, then the age to come must have begun. However, it was absolutely clear that the present age had not ceased, and that the final defeat of evil still remained in the future. The early Christians were thus forced to rethink their worldview, and concluded that in fact they were living in a period of overlap of the two ages, an overlap that would end when Jesus returned and the kingdom of God fully dawned. This can be diagrammed in the following way:

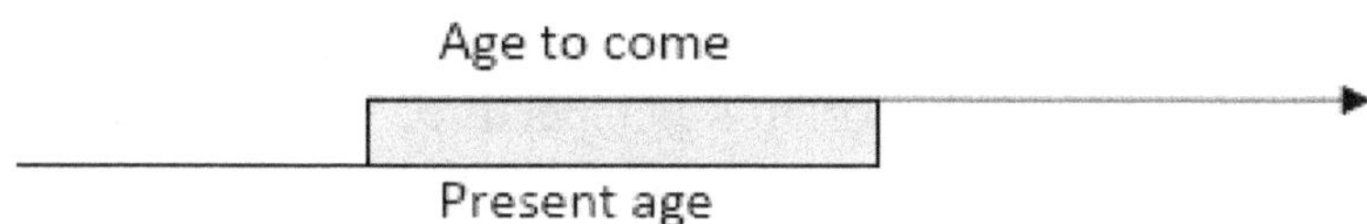

The resurrection of Jesus was viewed by the earliest Christians as an eschatological or "end-of-the-world" event, which happened slightly earlier than expected, but which was closely connected to the general resurrection, which could not be too far in the future, since it had already begun. It is for this reason that Jesus' resurrection is described in the New Testament as the "firstfruits" of the general "resurrection of the dead" (1 Corinthians 15:20). It is therefore not a belief that they could have simply come up with based on the assumptions they already had. No – something caused them to rethink their beliefs about God's kingdom, the end of the world, and God's timeline for human history, and what did this was presumably their conviction that Jesus had been raised from the dead. In other words, it was their conviction that something quite extraordinary and unexpected had happened to Jesus that led them to rethink their entire worldview, rather than their belief in Jesus' resurrection having been derived from the worldview and assumptions they already held.

As we have already seen, what precisely motivated them to believe that Jesus had been raised (the disappearance of the body, visions of angels, visions of Jesus himself, encounter with a living person they believed to be Jesus) is difficult if not impossible to say from a historian's perspective. What a historian *can*, indeed *must* say is that Christians did not simply invent beliefs to suit their tastes or their presuppositions. They must have had experiences that convinced them of something which would have seemed implausible based on beliefs that they already had: that a crucified man is the anointed one and Lord, that this one individual has been raised to eternal life as part of the final, eschatological resurrection, but nonetheless without the end of the world and the rest of the general resurrection taking place. The rise of Christian belief in the resurrection of Jesus does not necessarily require a "supernatural" explanation, but it does mean that something other than deception or even creativity is required to explain the facts.

Here it becomes important to ask what and how much Jesus may have said about his death and/or his coming vindication by God prior to the crucifixion, since this will affect whether it is plausible to explain subsequent Christian revisions of Jewish messianic and other beliefs in terms of what psychologists call "cognitive dissonance," that is, in terms of their rewriting some beliefs in order to preserve other core beliefs. But here too one must recognize that the post-

Easter Christians must have had a sufficiently strong conviction that Jesus is the Messiah and had risen from the dead for them to rewrite other fundamental beliefs in order to preserve these other core convictions. Most historians do not feel that Jesus said much if anything about his death before it happened, even though he must at the very least have been aware of the possibility that he might meet such an end, since his mentor John the Baptist had been arrested and killed. This topic, however, need not occupy too much of our time at this point. The authors of the New Testament Gospels, because they were persuaded that the crucifixion was part of God's plan, had no doubt Jesus *must* have been aware of it beforehand. But they present the disciples as not understanding except with hindsight, and being bewildered, perplexed and in despair after the crucifixion. This depiction of the leaders of the early Church is unlikely to have been invented and is thus historically credible. It is only after they have life-changing religious experiences of the sort we have discussed in this chapter that their outlook changes.

How Essential is the Resurrection to Christianity?

Could Christianity continue to exist without the doctrine of the resurrection as traditionally understood? Not only is it possible to answer in the affirmative, but we even appear to have an example (albeit only one) in the New Testament itself. The letter to the Hebrews presents Jesus as dying on the cross and then taking his sacrifice into the heavens, cleansing them and preparing the way for Christians to enter God's presence. There are no references to Jesus' resurrection using the standard Christian terminology found elsewhere in the New Testament (Hebrews 13:20 is the only reference to Jesus being "brought up from the dead," and it doesn't specify how or in what sense). Moreover, the logic of this letter's understanding of the work of Christ seems to leave no room for Jesus' return to a bodily existence. This reflects the influence of Platonic philosophy on this author, and so the evidence of Hebrews probably does not reflect what *most* ancient Christians thought about resurrection, atonement, and other issues. Nevertheless, it still raises some interesting questions. Does this suggest that the stories of the empty tomb and bodily appearances of Jesus were not universally known? Or that they were not so old and authoritative that one could not disagree with them? Or that there was some ambiguity as to their implications? Or could we imagine this author formulating a theology that ran roughshod over the basic tenets of what any of his intended readers would regard as the Christian faith?

Certainly the empty tomb is not crucial to the Christian faith, since it has nothing to do with what Christians have traditionally meant by resurrection. The Romans used to burn the bodies and scatter the ashes of

Christian martyrs, in an attempt to prevent them from being resurrected. I presume no Christian would suggest that the Romans could so easily thwart God's plans, and few today believe that, if there is to be a final resurrection of the dead, it will require God reassembling all the original molecules that made up one's body. This would be *resuscitation* rather than *resurrection*, a return to a bodily existence akin to our present one, rather than entry into the completely new manner of being that characterizes the age to come. And so the Christian belief that Jesus was not just brought back to life to die again, but was raised to eternal life, means that the fate of Jesus' body is ultimately irrelevant. The post-Easter Jesus is regarded by Christians as present to all believers everywhere, and is not felt to be limited spatially, unlike bodily existence as we now know it. When the New Testament Gospels depict Jesus appearing, locked doors do not present a hindrance for him appearing in a given room. So the focus of so much attention on the empty tomb is really something of a distraction, a side issue, as far as the resurrection of Jesus is concerned. The focus of the resurrection faith of Christians down the ages has not been a past event, but their experience of Jesus as a real, living presence in their lives.

It will always be possible to find other explanations for why Jesus' body was not in the tomb that Sunday morning. The most "natural" explanation is that "someone took the body," which is precisely what

John's Gospel tells us the disciples themselves initially thought, and Matthew's Gospel tells us that the Jewish authorities (and perhaps others) drew a similar conclusion. In view of the circumstances, this was a logical conclusion to draw, and one that came to mind more quickly than that the body had been raised to eternal life, indicating that the kingdom of God had dawned. The focus of the testimony of the early Christians about the resurrection seems to have been without exception "We have seen him" rather than "We found the tomb empty." An empty tomb can always be explained in various ways; it is only the experiences of the early Christians (and many others since) which indicate that something out of the ordinary may have happened.

Recognizing Jesus

As we have already mentioned, a historian cannot state with confidence precisely what the early Christians saw or even where they saw it. Luke's Gospel and Acts assume that the disciples remained in Jerusalem and saw Jesus there. Mark's Gospel promises that they will see Jesus *in Galilee*. Matthew has Jesus appear briefly in Jerusalem before the disciples head off to Galilee. And John's Gospel (in its final form, at any rate) seems to be trying to harmonize the two: it has appearances on two Sundays in Jerusalem, but also a subsequent appearance in Galilee. The Gospel tradition on where Jesus appeared to the Twelve is thus contradictory, and this raises a number of difficult questions about the history of the tradition of resurrection appearances.

Another feature that makes it problematic for historians to feel confident about what early Christians saw, and the nature of their resurrection experiences, is the fact that stories are told in which Jesus is not recognized, in which he apparently *did not look like Jesus* (see for example Luke 24:15-16; John 21:4, 12). In view of this perplexing element in the tradition, it is not surprising that some have suggested that either mistaken identity or even deception was involved. But as with any good conspiracy theory, these reconstructions are not so much interpretations of available evidence, as attempts to fill in the enormous holes in our knowledge by speculating around a few very small pieces of ambiguous information. Certainly in the earliest sources there is no mention of such uncertainty about the identity of Jesus. Yet even though such stories do not have much historical value and are laden with symbolism, nevertheless their presence in the Gospels makes matters even less clear-cut than they might otherwise be. In the story in Luke, it is in the context of the breaking of bread that Jesus is recognized, and this probably therefore represents a symbolic story, written from the perspective of Christian faith, of at least one way that Jesus is revealed to his followers in the period after Easter: in the celebration of the Lord's Supper.

The emphasis on Jesus having been resurrected in a tangible, physical body is clearly an apologetic motif. The stories about Jesus having eaten with the disciples are most likely late inventions, attempting to combat either the idea that Jesus only appeared to be human (called "docetism"), or the idea of a purely spiritual resurrection. But of course, the earliest evidence leaves the door wide open to just such an understanding: Jesus appears in locked rooms, disappears again, appears to individuals on the open road in a blaze of light and/or sound (depending on whether one follows Acts 9:7 or Acts 22:9). The earliest appearances of the risen Christ appear not to have clearly confirmed anything about the physicality of his nature. And so, in concluding this chapter, we may note what to some may be a disturbing possibility, but to others will seem an exciting prospect, namely that the experiences that persuaded the earliest Christians that Jesus was alive may have been precisely the same sorts of experiences that Christians continue to have even today.

Chapter 5
Conclusion: Beyond History

As one moves further and further away from the experience of the first Christians, one finds in early Christian literature an increasing emphasis on the *physicality* of Jesus' resurrection existence. This is, as we pointed out in the previous chapter, a response to what is known as *docetism*, which means the idea either that Jesus only appeared to be human, or that in his resurrection he was not physically present but only a spiritual reality. There was rightly seen to be a danger in denying the real bodily, physical, human existence of Jesus. Such denials were generally a result of the presupposition that material, bodily existence is a bad thing, which was problematic because it negated the goodness of creation affirmed in Genesis 1. Bodily resurrection, on the other hand, affirmed that God had indeed created the material world and declared it "good." Eternal life is in some sense bodily, according to at least most of the New Testament authors, and this explicitly counters the view of eternal life as *escape from the body*, a departure from the physical world.

Whether that body should be thought of in *physical* terms was and is another question.

There is something profoundly ironic about the fact that, in contemporary Christianity, one most frequently encounters, on the one hand, a strong emphasis on Jesus having risen physically, and yet on the other hand, eternal life is thought of in terms of "going to heaven when I die." The latter view of the afterlife was precisely the one that the New Testament authors seem to have been concerned to counter, since it viewed the material world as something negative to be escaped from, rather than something that God would transform in the age to come. It makes little sense if any to hold to the resurrection of Jesus as a unique event in this way, utterly disconnected from one's more general view of the afterlife, rather than as the first instance of something that will experienced by all. It thus seems that, in strictly pragmatic terms, resurrection is not in fact absolutely essential to Christianity, since many Christians have already abandoned it in practice as part of their expectation about afterlife. If it makes sense to regard eternal life as something non-bodily, then surely the appropriate action is to regard Jesus as having entered eternal life in precisely the same way and same form as will eventually happen to all. This is the central New Testament pattern, with Jesus as the forerunner and firstfruits, having already undergone what will happen to the rest of God's people when the kingdom fully dawns.

The danger in taking this path, however, is one that already existed in the early Church, but which seems no less a concern today. As we have already hinted above, among those who denied the physicality of Jesus' resurrection, or who denied the concept of resurrection altogether, the main reason for doing so was a view of physical existence as something negative. The material world was regarded as evil, and the best one could hope for was to have one's spirit escape from it. For Christians, however, such a viewpoint involved a fundamental denial of the doctrine of creation, which maintains that God is good and has created a physical universe that is good, as affirmed in Genesis 1. Indeed, those groups that denied a physical resurrection often also denied that the God of Jesus Christ, the highest God, was the same God who is depicted as creating the universe in the Jewish Scriptures. Although few Christians today adhere to this particular set of doctrines (usually referred to as Gnosticism), it is still a common viewpoint in certain streams of Christianity to consider that the physical world is doomed to imminent destruction, and thus it makes no sense to concern oneself with the environment, for instance, or even to plant a tree. Apart from the irony of such short sightedness among adherents of a religion that has been around for some 2,000 years, this viewpoint denies the Biblical teaching that there will be a new heavens and a new earth, with new bodies for those who participate in the life of the age to come. In the Bible, the emphasis is on a *transformation* of creation, and not simply its destruction. If one lets go of the idea of resurrection, the danger is that a negative view of bodily existence will result. This is not to suggest that the solution is to move to the other extreme, to an over-emphasis on the physicality of Jesus' resurrection. In the writings of Paul, not only is Jesus' resurrection body not merely flesh and blood, it is not even merely individual. In Paul's letters he refers on more than one occasion to the Church as the "body of Christ," and one gets the very strong impression that for him this is more than "just a metaphor." And of course, in asking questions about Christian doctrine today, it is appropriate to include in the mix of data not only the varied Biblical statements on the subject, but the ways in which we understand human persons, including data from the natural sciences and from psychology.

Questions about the resurrection as a Christian doctrine, or about eternal life in general, cannot be answered by historical study alone, even though historical study has much to say that is relevant, as do the sciences and other fields of human knowledge. Nor is the idea of eternal life something that one can *demonstrate* from historical evidence (as we've seen throughout this book), or on other grounds such as scientific ones. This is not surprising, even from a Biblical perspective. Genesis 2-3 presents human beings as created sharing in mortality just like the rest of life on earth. It is not that humans are created immortal in that famous Biblical story; on the contrary, they are graciously allowed access to the tree of life and thus immortality, and they lose access to the gift when exiled from the Garden of Eden. The Bible itself therefore regards eternal life as a divine gift rather than an inherent possession of human beings. When one couples this with the understanding of human beings as psychosomatic unities, about which the Bible (for the most part, at least) and modern science agree, it becomes clear that one cannot simply take for granted an understanding of eternal life in terms of the departure of an immortal soul, regarded as the home of one's personality, memories, and identity. If such elements of our existence are indeed to be preserved, it must be something that God graciously does. How this might be accomplished is something we cannot answer, but one can certainly find analogies that are useful, and metaphors that make these ideas more intelligible to a contemporary audience. For example, I have long been struck by the parallels between Evangelical religious language and computing terminology in speaking about being "saved" or "lost." The image of God, as it were, "downloading" the things that make us *us*, may or may not correspond to something that actually happens, but all religious language is inherently metaphorical and symbolic, and this contemporary imagery may be a useful way of updating some of the classic imagery Christians have tended to use in discussing this subject.

But does it make sense to think of eternal life in terms of the persistence for all time of my own personality, my own consciousness, and my own *ego*? Such an idea, however popular, is difficult to maintain, especially when one tries to imagine how there might be any genuine continuity in our personalities and memories after the passing of eons. Even the continuity of our own existence and personality over a human lifespan is not a straightforward matter, since at no point are we consciously aware of all the events and experiences that have shaped us. And of course, if in the afterlife people *did* remember everything that ever happened to them, that in itself would make us different persons to the ones were are in the human existence we experience from day to day. Thus, to think in terms of a unified persistent "ego" may be an unhelpful way of envisaging eternal life. But in addition to such practical concerns, there is good reason to ask whether the emphasis on afterlife and rewards found in much contemporary Christianity is not in fact spiritually unhealthy.

This last statement may seem odd, and to some may even seem unthinkable, so let me clarify my meaning. Belief in an afterlife was not always a part of Jewish belief, nor was the view that God will right injustices committed in this life by meting out rewards and punishments after death. One can read early prophetic books like Amos and Hosea, the Book of Proverbs and other wisdom literature, and the entire

Pentateuch or Torah (the first five books of the Bible) without ever encountering such ideas. In most of the literature of the Jewish Scriptures, what Christians call the "Old Testament," one finds instead a strong belief that rewards and punishments are apportioned in *this life*, *within* human history rather than *beyond* it. For most Christians today, belief in the afterlife is so central that it seems hard to believe *any* religion could fail to focus on it, much less the religious tradition of earlier parts of our own Bible. Yet all one has to do is to read these books in order to see that this is in fact the case.

Belief in rewards in the afterlife appears to have arisen in response to the crisis of the persecution the Jewish people experienced during the reign of the Syrian king Antiochus Epiphanes, the story of which is told in the books of Maccabees in Catholic and Orthodox Bibles. The end of this period of persecution, and the rededication of the Temple which had been desecrated in the process, is commemorated in the festival of Hanukkah. Of course, the "problem of evil" (or in other words, the problem of why, if God is good and all-powerful, bad things happen to good people) had long been recognized and discussed. However, the experiences of this period stretched solutions that had previously been adequate to beyond their breaking point. This is because it was precisely those who were seeking to obey God's laws and be faithful to God who were singled out for persecution and death. To continue to affirm the goodness of God, it was felt necessary to assert that somehow God would overrule the human authorities that had made martyrs of those devoted to him. God, it was concluded, would reward them beyond death.

Clearly this basis for resurrection is closely connected to Christian faith in the resurrection of Jesus. For Christians, affirming the resurrection means and has always meant affirming that while human rulers had condemned and executed Jesus, God has overturned their verdict and has vindicated Jesus even beyond death. There is nothing in the conclusions of historical study or scientific that makes such language seem either appropriate or inappropriate. Such affirmations are not about history but about theology. What does seem problematic, however, is the way in which resurrection, understood in terms of survival of human individuals beyond death, reinforces certain negative aspects of our culture today.

Our society is highly individualistic, and in many respects encourages self-centeredness. Such a diagnosis of our culture is not a new one. Yet in the context of such a cultural setting, faith in God as one who raises the dead and rewards those faithful to God often gets transformed into cocky assertions about one's own immortality. More often than not, in the context of American culture in particular, it becomes a self-centered focus on attaining rewards in heaven, one that seems to be in tension with the Bible's emphasis on self denial, humility, and utter dependence on God.

What has gone wrong? It seems to me that perhaps the error is in focusing on afterlife and rewards rather than on God, and in emphasizing certainty about the hereafter rather than divine justice or dependence on God. Affirming the resurrection ought not to be an expression of absolute certainty, as though anyone alive today could claim either to have touched the resurrection body of Jesus, or to know beyond a shadow of a doubt that someone else had done so. It is more appropriate, not only in the light of historical inquiry but also in light of the core emphases in the Bible, to speak of *resurrection faith*, which does not mean believing without evidence in the resurrection as something that has happened and will happen, but rather means trusting in the God who is capable of rescuing even from death. This should be the heart of resurrection faith: trust and hope in God rather than arrogant self-assuredness.

An excessive focus on the afterlife has at times had the ironic effect of leading Christians to ignore those very aspects of human existence that led to the formation of the doctrine in the first place. It was the conviction that God hates injustice that led those who did not see injustice being eliminated in this life to affirm that God would surely do it in another. Yet nowadays one is more likely to find Christians using the hope of eternal life as a basis for *ignoring* injustice. Only God can eliminate injustice, we are often told, and so the appropriate response from human beings is to sit tight and wait for God to act. Such statements run counter to much teaching in the Bible, and yet there are writings (particularly in the New Testament) that can indeed seem to give this impression.

As we reflect on this topic, we should not ignore the fundamental differences between the context of the New Testament authors and our own. On the one hand, they were not living in a democracy in which they had the potential to change society without resorting to violent means. In a democratic context in which we are invited to influence society and participate in government, to simply parrot the words of the New Testament authors who lived in a dictatorship is a mistake. Surely the appropriate question to ask is "What would Jesus (and his followers) do if they had lived in our context?" and not merely "What did they do in theirs?" Also not to be overlooked is the fact that belief in the resurrection of Jesus was part of the early Christians' belief that the end of the world was at hand, that the kingdom of God was arriving in all its fullness. Certainly none of the earliest New Testament authors could have imagined that millennia would pass and human history would still be continuing. If we continue to simply assert that "the end is near" even when in the process we are stretching the meaning of those words past their breaking point, we are not being faithful to the witness of the New Testament, because later New Testament authors, confronted with the fact that the end of the world and the second coming of Jesus did not occur as swiftly as had been anticipated, gave these matters further thought and revised their viewpoint. This is what we see in chapter 21 of Luke's Gospel, for example, when he rewrites the end-times discourse in Mark 13, so that it refers almost entirely to the destruction of Jerusalem, and so that predicting that "the end is near," instead of being the meaning of Jesus' words, is a sign that one is a false prophet (compare in particular Luke 21:8 with its parallel in Mark 13:6). Similarly, throughout John's Gospel we find those things that were anticipated at the end of history being affirmed as present realities: judgment has already taken place (John 3:16-18), resurrection and eternal life are present experiences (John 11:23-26), the Son (together with the Father and the Spirit) have already returned spiritually to dwell with us (e.g. John 14:23).

So much Christianity in our time suffers from this one overarching flaw: we tend to repeat the *words* of the New Testament authors, while altogether ignoring *what they were doing* when they wrote those words. If we truly want to take the New Testament authors as models of Christian discipleship, we should be following their example in being willing to rethink and rewrite in response to new information and changing circumstances. That is a truly *Biblical* Christianity, since it takes fully seriously the differences between Biblical writings and the development between them, rather than forcing their divergent perspectives into the idolatrous straightjacket of a doctrine of Biblical inerrancy. Historically, Christian theologians have left room for the concept of "progressive revelation," which means in essence that sometimes things became clearer later that were not clear earlier, and views and understandings changed and developed with time.

This should not, however, be taken to mean that we focus on later writings and ignore earlier ones, as though what is written later not only supplements and goes beyond but automatically invalidates or supplants earlier writings. Indeed, our present discussion could be understood as an attempt to take seriously, from a Christian perspective, writings like Ecclesiastes (which discusses the afterlife only to question it, in 3:18-22 for example) and the Book of Job. The key message of the Book of Job is not to offer a solution to the problem of evil, but to offer a critique of human claims to know how to resolve it. Throughout the book, Job's "friends" make affirmations about the goodness of God which are thoroughly orthodox and often sound like they are quotes straight out of the book of Proverbs. Job, on the other hand, affirms that his own experience shows the inadequacy of traditional wisdom, at least as applied to his own case. None of the characters in the book learn of the heavenly wager depicted in chapters 1-2. When God appears at the end of the book, it is not to explain why Job is suffering, but to challenge human claims to wisdom and understanding, or at least claims to be able to wrap up God and God's relationship to the world in a nice neat package or simple equation.

The bigger question the book raises, however, is found in Job 1:9, where it asks about Job's motives for serving God. In a world in which the righteous always prosper and the wicked always perish, where is there room for selfless devotion to God? The emphasis placed on rewards and punishment in the afterlife within Christianity is in serious danger of undermining the message of Job and the possibility of loving God and others in a way that is not ultimately motivated by self-interest. Focus on God as one who is capable of granting eternal life as a gift, but also leaving such matters thoroughly in God's hands, seems like a more appropriate attitude, leaving room for us to act for the good of others without this being viewed simply as a means to acquire "treasure in heaven." Perhaps this shift of emphasis could help to heal the persistent self-centeredness that has so infected American Christianity as to leave us unable to critique and challenge this dominant cultural value. It might also allow us to embrace in positive ways the other forms of "afterlife" that are important in earlier writings within the Bible: the legacy we leave to our children and to the world around us, both in terms of the way we are remembered as individuals, but also in terms of our positive influence and impact in making the world a better place than it was before we arrived.

Resurrection faith, we have suggested in this book, was not born from historical deductions regarding the whereabouts of a body, but from life-transforming religious experiences. For those of us who have had such experiences, faith is not primarily (if at all) a matter of doctrines but of what we can only speak of in symbolic terms as a life-transforming *relationship* to the ultimate. When the focus of Christian faith is placed there, then the possibility of keeping faith about *humble trust* rather than *arrogant claims to certainty* becomes realistic. There appear to be two major approaches to matters of faith which cut across distinctions not only of denomination but of religion as well. For some, religion is about confidently knowing; for others, it is about meekly acknowledging the inadequacy of our human knowledge. For some, it is about affirmations in words; for others, it is about an experience that transcends anything to which human words could ever do justice. For those in the latter category, the idea that this experience of the divine, this enjoyment of God, this relationship with God may not end with death seems entirely feasible. But the basis for such a statement is not found in history. On the contrary, if you ask me how (or in what sense) "I know he lives," the answer will be, as Ackley's famous hymn says, "he lives within my heart."

www.ingramcontent.com/pod-product-compliance
Lightning Source LLC
La Vergne TN
LVHW020633100826
845148LV00012B/2171

* 9 7 8 1 6 6 6 7 8 4 1 5 2 *